02/13/99

GLASGOW
the BEST!
THE ONE TRUE GUIDE

Peter Irvine
and
Graeme Kelling

HarperCollins*Publishers*

To Pat Lally
Always Miles Better

HarperCollins Publishers
P.O. Box, Glasgow G4 0NB

First published 1998

Reprint 10 9 8 7 6 5 4 3 2 1 0

© Peter Irvine, 1998
Photographs © The Printer's Devil, except those on pages 28 (© Yes),
33 (© Stravaigin) and 60 (© Fratelli Sarti), 1998

Cover photograph: The People's Palace, Glasgow Green (The Printer's Devil)

ISBN 0 00 472153 5

A catalogue record for this book is available from the British Library

Printed and bound in Great Britain by the Bath Press

CONTENTS

WHERE TO DRINK

WHERE TO GO IN TOWN

WHERE TO GO OUT OF TOWN

The telephone code for Glasgow is 0141

INTRODUCTION

Welcome to the first edition of this city handbook extracted and updated from *Scotland the Best!* which, now in its fourth edition, has proven to be the most popular independent guide to our incredible country. Coming out every two years, it's the one the Scots use themselves, an insider guide written like this one by people who know and love their subject. Glasgow is a big subject: here it has been reduced and condensed so that only the good information is included. You should need no other guide, but please let us know what you think – we thrive on feedback.

As you become familiar with *Glasgow the Best!*, you will see that it is not quite like other guides. It doesn't give you lots of orientation information (it assumes you can negotiate your own arrival and can follow universal rules for survival in a new city) and you may need to consult a proper map (available free along with loads of other bumf from the Tourist Information Centres at the airport and at 35 St Vincent St downtown) since our maps are very diagrammatic. What it does give you in a broad range of categories is the best of what Glasgow (and its immediate area) has to offer. We are highly selective and do not give all the options – only the best places. This includes the obvious, like the Burrell Collection, as well as the obscure, but nowhere is listed just because it's there – if it's mediocre, we ignore it. So, we're not too horrible about anyone – this is a positive book.

Although the selection process is undertaken by us, many people are consulted before choices are made and everywhere has been visited and sampled. We hope we are saving you the bother of having a less than satisfactory experience and we stand by all our recommendations. But nobody pays for inclusion, there are no ads, no subscriptions and no sponsorship. We do not employ a rigid set of standards and we tolerate idiosyncrasy because we'd rather have integrity and authenticity than mere amenity. Quality and attitude are what we recognize and want to bring to your attention. Service and atmosphere, attention to detail and value for money are all evaluated in making our decisions. This guide is written for you – not them – and not the 'industry'.

We want you to know that Glasgow is one of the best cities on earth.

Enjoy it!

A DECLARATION OF FALLIBILITY

This guide is 'true', but it may not always be absolutely accurate. Since this may seem like a contradiction in terms, I should explain. *Glasgow the Best!* is a handbook of information about all the 'best' places in Glasgow. 'Best', you will understand, is a subjective term; it means 'best' according to what we think. Needless to say, there seem to be a lot of readers who agree with this judgement, and even if you don't you may see that I and my associates have gone to some efforts to reach our assertions. It's intended to be obvious that we are conveying opinions and impressions. They're true because the motives are true; we believe in what we are saying. We take no bribes and we have no vested interest in any of the places recommended, other than that we do talk things up and shamelessly proclaim the places we like or admire.

We hope it's plain where the facts end and the opinions begin. In guidebooks this is not always the case. However, it's with 'the facts' that inconsistencies may appear. We try to give accurate and clear directions explaining how to find a place and basic details that might be useful. This information is gleaned from a variety of sources and may be supplied by the establishment concerned. We do try to verify everything usually by visiting but things change and since nowhere we recommend has solicited their inclusion – we don't run copy past them – inaccuracies may occur. We hope that there aren't any, or many, but we may not find out until you let us know. We'd appreciate it if you would, so we can fix it for the next edition.

HOW TO USE THIS BOOK

There are three ways to use this book:

1. There's a straightforward index at the back. If you know somewhere already (and it's any good) you should find it here. Numbers refer to page numbers.

2. The book can be used by categories, e.g. you can look up the best French restaurants or the best pubs with outdoor drinking. Each entry has an item number in the outside margin. These are in numerical order and allow easy cross-referencing.

Categories are in groups, e.g. Where to Stay, Where to Eat. Each section has a map.

3. You can start with the maps and see how individual items are located, how they are grouped together, what's available in a particular area or what restaurants are recommended near where you are staying, for example.

The maps cover the city centre only and are not to scale. They are intended to be diagrammatic only. Each entry has a map reference which can be found beneath the item number in the border. If an item is out of the centre an arrow indicates its direction off the map. In the border this is denoted by an x, e.g. xD4 means 'Off the map at square D4'.

THE CELTIC CROSSES

Although everything listed in the book is notable and remarkable in some way, there are places that are outstanding even in this superlative company. Instead of marking them with a rosette or a star, they have been 'awarded' a Celtic cross symbol, the traditional Scottish version of the cross.

♰ Among the very best in Scotland

♰ ♰ Among the best (of its type) in the UK

♰ ♰ ♰ Among the best (of its type) in the world, or simply unique

A NOTE ON CATEGORIES

The book is arranged in five categories: Where to Stay; Where to Eat; Where to Drink; Where to Go (for general activities) in Town; and Where to Go out of Town. Within these five sections, categories range from the (mainly) very expensive, e.g. Best Hotels, to the fairly cheap, e.g. Best Hostels. The final section, Where to Go out of Town, lists places near to the city, easily reached by car or public transport and for a range of interests. Like most of the other items in *Glasgow the Best!*, these have been extracted from *Scotland the Best!*, which covers the whole of the country.

THE CODES

1. The Item Code

At the outside margin of every item is a code which will enable you to find it on a map. Thus **231** *E3* should be read as follows: **231** is the item number, listed in a simple consecutive order; *E3* is the map coordinate, to help pinpoint the item's location on the map grid. A coordinate such as *xA4* indicates that the item can be reached by leaving the map at grid reference *A4*.

2. The Hotel Codes

Below each hotel recommended is a band of codes as follows:

20RMS   JAN-DEC   T/T   PETS   CC   KIDS   TOS   LOTS

20RMS   means the hotel has 20 bedrooms in total. No differentiation is made as to the type of room. Most hotels will offer twin rooms as singles or put extra beds in doubles if required. This code merely gives an impression of size.

JAN-DEC   means the hotel is open all year round. APR-OCT means approximately from the beginning of April to the end of October.

T/T   refers to the facilities: T/ means there are direct-dial phones in the bedrooms, while /T means there are TVs in the bedrooms.

PETS   means the hotel accepts dogs and other pets, probably under certain conditions (e.g. pets should be kept in the bedroom). It's usually best to check first.

XPETS   indicates that the hotel does not generally accept pets.

CC   means the hotel accepts major credit cards (e.g. Access and Visa).

XCC   mcans the hotel does not accept major credit cards.

KIDS   indicates children are welcome and special provisions/rates may be available.

XKIDS   does not necessarily mean that children are not able to accompany their parents, only that special provisions/rates are not usually made. Check by phone.

TOS   means the hotel is part of the Taste of Scotland scheme and has been selected for having a menu which features imaginative cooking using Scottish ingredients. The Taste of Scotland produces an annual guide of members.

LOTS   Rooms which cost more than £60 per night per person. The theory is that if you can afford over £120 a room, it doesn't matter too much if it's £125 or £150. Other price bands are:

EXP   Expensive: £50-60 per person.

MED.EXP   Medium (expensive): £38-50.

MED.INX   Medium (inexpensive): £28-38.

INX   Inexpensive: £20-28.

CHP   Cheap: less than £20.

Rates are per person per night. They are worked out by halving the published average rate for a twin room in high season and should be used only to give an impression of cost. They are based on 1997 prices. Add between £2 and £5 per year, though the band should stay the same unless the hotel undergoes improvements.

3. The Restaurant Code

Found at the bottom right of all restaurant entries. It refers to the price of an average dinner per person with a starter, a main course and a dessert. It doesn't include wine, coffee or extras.

EXP   Expensive: more than £30.

MED   Medium: £20-30.

INX   Inexpensive: £12-20.

CHP   Cheap: less than £12.

These are based on 1997 rates. With inflation, the relatige price bands should stay about the same.

4. The Walk Codes

A number of walks are described in the book. Below each walk is a band of codes as follows:

2-10km CIRC BIKE 1-A-1

2-10km   means the walk(s) described may vary in length from 2km to 10km.

CIRC   means the walk can be circular, while XCIRC shows the walk is not circular and you must return more or less by the way you came.

BIKE   indicates the walk has a path which is suitable for ordinary bikes.

XBIKE   means the walk is not suitable for, or does not permit, cycling.

MTBIKE   means the track is suitable for mountain or all-terrain bikes.

The 1-A-1 Code

First number (1, 2, 3) indicates how easy the walk is.

1 the walk is easy; 2 medium difficulty, e.g. standard hillwalking, not dangerous nor requiring special knowledge or equipment; 3 difficult: care, preparation and a map are needed.

The letters (A, B, C) indicate how easy it is to find the path.

A the route is easy to find. The way is either marked or otherwise obvious; B the route is not very obvious, but you'll get there; C you will need a map and preparation or a guide.

The last number (1, 2, 3) indicates what to wear on your feet.

1   ordinary outdoor shoes, including trainers, are probably OK unless the ground is very wet; 2 you will need walking boots; 3 you will need serious walking or hiking boots.

Apart from the designated walks, the 1-A-1 code is employed wherever there is more than a short stroll required to get somewhere, e.g. a waterfall or a monument. The code appears at the bottom-right corner of the item.

LIST OF ABBREVIATIONS

As well as codes and because of obvious space limitations, a personal shorthand and ad hoc abbreviation system has had to be created. I'm the first to admit some may be annoying, especially 'restau' for restaurant, but it's a long word and it comes up often. The others which are used are:

accom	accommodation	incl	including
adj	adjacent	inexp	inexpensive
admn	admission	info	information
app	approach	jnct	junction
approx	approximately	L	loch
atmos	atmosphere	LO	last orders
av	average	min(s)	minute(s)
ave	avenue	N	north
AYR	all year round	no smk	no smoking
bedrms	bedrooms	nr	near
betw	between	NTS	National Trust for Scotland
br	bridge		
BYOB	bring your own bottle	o/look(s)	overlook(s)/ing
		opp	opposite
cl	closes/closed	o/side	outside
cres	crescent	pl	place
dining-rm	dining-room	poss	possible
dr	drive	pt	point/port
E	east	R	river
Edin	Edinburgh	r/bout	roundabout
esp	especially	rd	road
excl	excluding	refurb	refurbished/ment
exhib(s)	exhibition(s)	restau	restaurant
exp	expensive	rm(s)	room(s)
facs	facilities	rt	right
ft	fort	S	south
Glas	Glasgow	sq	square
gr	great	st	street
grd(s)	garden(s)	stn	station
hr(s)	hour(s)	SYHA	Scottish Youth Hostels Association
HS	Historic Scotland		

terr	terrace	v	very
TO	tourist information office	vac	vacation
t/off	turn-off	vegn	vegetarian
trad	traditional	W	west
tratt	trattoria	w/end(s)	weekend(s)
univ	university	yr(s)	year(s)

WHERE TO STAY

Architectural splendour in St Vincent St

THE BEST HOTELS

✝ ✝ **ONE DEVONSHIRE GARDENS:** 339 2001. 1 Devonshire Grds. Off Gr Western Rd (the A82 W to Dumbarton), to arrive by car you have to go round the back. 3 separate houses in leafy Victorian terr, and after accolades and write-ups galore, the most notable urban hotel in Scotland. It's all down to detail and service, fab fixtures and fabrics: it's all down to DESIGN and Ken McCulloch. Every rm is different but all have the things that we modern travellers look out for: CD players, big beds, huge baths, deep baths, deep carpets/ towels/curtains (but could it be the breakfast OJ was – help ma boab – out of a carton?). Some Ralph Lauren rms; the supersuites all in house 3 (rms 21, 27, 28) if you're Pavarotti or just celebrating. Restau a foodie experience in itself (49/BEST RESTAUS).   27RMS JAN-DEC T/T PETS CC KIDS LOTS

1
xB1

✝ **THE MALMAISON:** 572 1000. 278 W George St. Sister hotel of the one in Edin and same team as One Devonshire *(see above)* so no surprise that this is an outstanding hotel. The recent expansion, utilising the adj building, has more than tripled the accom, and the addition of the Café Mal downstairs has created a cool, sky-lit area in contrast to the woody clubbiness of the brasserie next door (60/BEST BISTROS). An improvement on what was already pretty good to begin with. Well proportioned rms (some suites), with CDs, cable, etc. Stylish excellence.
    73RMS JAN-DEC T/T XPETS CC KIDS MED.EXP

2
C3

✝ **THE DEVONSHIRE HOTEL:** 339 7878. 5 Devonshire Grds. Confusingly perhaps for first-time visitors, this similarly sumptuous town house hotel is at the other end of the short block containing One Devonshire *(see above)*. I say 'similarly' (pictures, plants, atmos, etc), but it is less de luxe, less designey and some may find more effortless. Dining for residents only. All bedrms delightfully different.   14RMS JAN-DEC T/T PETS CC KIDS LOTS

3
xB1

✝ **NAIRN'S:** 353 0707. 13 Woodside Cres, nr Charing Cross. 4 rms above Nick Nairn's eponymous restau and clearly one of the best places in town to have breakfast (and dinner) (46/BEST RESTAUS). Each rm v individual with different themes (one definitely more S&M than M&S), but all with good light and good bathrms.   4RMS JAN-DEC T/T XPETS CC KIDS EXP

4
B2

GLASGOW HILTON: 204 5555. 1 William St. App from the M8 slip rd or from city centre via Waterloo St. It has a forbidding Fritz

5
C3

Lang/Metropolis appearance which isn't really dispelled once inside. The clean lines of the atrium/lobby and the ubiquitous theme bar and bistro off it increase the sensation of being on a huge and expensive film set. But, hotel it is, and one of the best in the town with good service and appointments. Japanese people made esp welcome. Cameron's, the hotel's main restau, is present and correct; Minsky's bistro and Raffles bar not too special.

319RMS JAN-DEC T/T PETS CC KIDS LOTS

6
C3

THE MARRIOTT: 226 5577. 500 Argyle St, nr motorway. Modern and functional business hotel where parking is a test for the nerves. Nevertheless, there's a calm, helpful attitude from the staff inside; for further de-stressing you can hypnotize yourself by watching the soundless traffic on the Kingston br o/side; or there's a pool to lap. No-smk floors. 298RMS JAN-DEC T/T PETS CC KIDS LOTS

7
D3

THE COPTHORNE: 332 6711. 50 George Sq. Situated on the sq which is the municipal heart of the city and next to Queen St Stn (trains to Edin and pts NE), Glas will be going on all about you and there's a conservatory terr, serving breakfast and afternoon tea, from which to watch. Bedrms vary greatly; some perhaps over-done. Busy brasserie. 141RMS JAN-DEC T/T PETS CC KIDS LOTS

8
A4

THE MOAT HOUSE: 306 9988. Congress Rd. Beside the SECC, on the Clyde, this towering, glass monument to the 1980s feels like it's in a constant state of 'siege readiness'. The Marine Restau, in the lobby, has a good reputation and ring-side seating for river-gazing. Somewhat removed from city centre (about 3km but you would-n't want to walk), it's esp handy for SECC and Armadillo goings-on. 282RMS JAN-DEC T/T PETS CC KIDS LOTS

9
D3

THE CENTRAL HOTEL: 221 9680. Gordon St. Once the last word in gracious living, the elegance is now a little faded, although a cer-tain atmos still remains in the sweep of the staircase and in the grandiose public rms. Rms are individual and you're at the hub of a gr city. Taxis easy to find, parking less so. New leisure centre.

221RMS JAN-DEC T/T PETS CC KIDS EXP

10
A3

KELVIN PARK LORNE: 314 9955. 923 Sauchiehall St. By no means in the superluxe league, but included because many of the rms, esp the suites, are individualistic, often rather grand. Location is handy for the W End (galleries/ restaus/Kelvingrove Park).

99RMS JAN-DEC T/T PETS CC KIDS EXP

WEST END

GREAT WESTERN ROAD

Kelvingrove Park

Charing Cross

SOUTH SIDE

River Clyde

Glasgow Green

SECC

1,3

4

5

6

10

8

9

2

7

A — E

1 — 5

M8

SYDES ROAD
DUMBARTON RD
GREAT WESTERN ROAD
WOODLANDS ROAD
ARGYLE STREET
SAUCHIEHALL STREET
BERKELEY STREET
ST VINCENT STREET
CLYDESIDE EXPRESSWAY
River Clyde
PAISLEY ROAD WEST
POLLOKSHIELDS
GORBALS STREET
BALLATER STREET
GALLOWGATE
SALTMARKET
HIGH STREET
Clyde Street
BROOMIELAW
CENTRAL STATION
QUEEN STREET STATION
BUCHANAN BUS STATION
MERCHANT CITY
ST ENOCH SHOPPING CENTRE

THE BEST
INEXPENSIVE HOTELS

11
E3

✚ **CATHEDRAL HOUSE:** 552 3519. 28-32 Cathedral Sq/John Knox St. Next to the Cathedral (some rms o/look) and close to the Merchant City, this detached old building has been tastefully refurbed and converted into a café-bar (with occasional live music), a separate restau (Fri-Sat at time of going to press) and comfortable bedrms above. Discreet and informal hospitality for the traveller; much as it always has been here, in the ancient heart of the city.   7RMS   JAN-DEC   T/T   PETS   CC   KIDS   MED.EXP

12
xB1

✚ **THE TOWN HOUSE:** 357 0862. 4 Hughenden Terr. Quiet st off Gr Western Rd via Hyndland Rd, o/looking the cricket grounds. These spacious rms have been faithfully restored and even if you don't happen to live in a well-appointed town house on a gracious terr yourself, you'll feel at home here. Close to the W End.   10RMS   JAN-DEC   T/T   XPETS   CC   KIDS   MED.INX

13
C3

✚ **CHARING CROSS TOWER:** 221 1000. 10 Elmbank Grds, above Charing Cross Stn. Once an office block, now a vast city-centre budget hotel, with no frills and no pretence, but a v adequate rm for the night – I mean it's not a pile of charm and you wouldn't want to spend your holidays here, but its functionalism, anonymity and urban melancholy make it a Euro-Glas must. M8 rms less quiet.   276RMS   JAN-DEC   T/T   XPETS   CC   KIDS   MED.INX

14
E4

✚ **THE BRUNSWICK:** 552 0001. 104-108 Brunswick St. V contemporary, minimalist hotel in Merchant City. Bright and cheerful rms economically designed to make use of space; low Japanese-style beds. Good base for nocturnal forays into pub and club land. Restau has had mixed response, but breakfast v pleasant. Check the Penthouse.   8RMS   JAN-DEC   T/T   XPETS   CC   KIDS   MED.EXP

15
E4

✚ **RAB HA'S:** 572 0400. 83 Hutcheson St. Rms above a pub (231/PUB FOOD) in the urban heart of the Merchant City that have had a recent overhaul; new central-heating system, etc. Good place to get plumbed into Glas! Good food.
          4RMS   JAN-DEC   T/T   PETS   CC   XKIDS   MED.INX

16
D4

✚ **THE COURTYARD HOTEL:** 552 2424. 52 Virginia St. Conversion of the old Tobacco Merchants house (in Merchant City) that has managed to retain the original staircase (ask the porter to take your bags, there's no lift). Surprisingly quiet area nr shops and in emerging gay zone.   34RMS JAN-DEC T/T PETS CC KIDS CHP

BABBITY BOWSTER: 552 5055. 16-18 Blackfriars St. This carefully renovated, late 18th-century town house was pivotal in the rede-velopment of the Merchant City. Renowned for its hospitality; bar (215/real-ale pubs, 230/pub food) and beer grd, Schottische restau upstairs and simple accom above. A welcoming howff, with Culture thrown in. 6RMS JAN-DEC X/X XPETS CC XKIDS MED.INX

17
E4

WICKETS HOTEL: 334 9334. 52 Fortrose St. Probably best app via Dumbarton Rd, turning up Peel St before railway br. O/looking W of Scotland Cricket Ground, this family-run hotel has been a Kelvinside secret for yrs. Decent rms, conservatory restau and a beer grd made for long summer afternoons (245/DRINKING OUT-DOORS). 10RMS JAN-DEC T/T PETS CC KIDS MED.INX

18
xA2

KIRKLEE: 334 5555. 11 Kensington Gate. The Stevens keep a tidy house and most notably a tidy grd in this leafy suburb nr Botanics and Byres Rd. 9RMS JAN-DEC T/T XPETS CC KIDS MED.INX

19
xA1

THE WHITE HOUSE: 339 9375. 12 Cleveden Cres. Not really a hotel, more self-catering apartments nr Botanics. V civilised alternative, esp if there are a few of you or you are staying a week.
8UNITS JAN-DEC T/T PETS CC KIDS MED.INX

20
xA1

NUMBER 52 CHARLOTTE STREET: 553 1941. Serviced apartments in superb conversion of the one remaining Georgian town house in historic (now decimated) st betw the Barrows Market and Glas Green. V good rates for bedrm/lounge/kitchen; everything but breakfast. 6RMS JAN-DEC X/T XPETS CC KIDS MED.INX

21
E4

THE VICTORIAN HOUSE: 332 0129. 214 Renfrew St. Expansive guest-house which has swallowed up adj houses in hill-top terr behind Sauchiehall St nr Art School (314/MACKINTOSH). Basic accom. Rms without facs cheaper but bathrms can be a floor away. Location is the appeal. 36RMS JAN-DEC X/T PETS CC KIDS INX

22
C2

RENNIE MACKINTOSH HOTEL: 333 9992. 218-220 Renfrew St. Taking advantage of the upcoming Year of Architecture in 1999, this new hotel, and its partner, the **GREEK THOMSON:** 332 6556, at 140 Elderslie St, have cheekily borrowed the names of 2 of Glasgow's most famous sons. The Mockintosh isn't too overbearing, the ser-vice is friendly and helpful, and there's alfresco breakfasting in the summer. 24/17RMS JAN-DEC T/T X/PETS CC KIDS INX

23
C2, B3

THE BEST HOSTELS

The SYH(A) is the Scottish Youth Hostel Association, of which you have to be a member (or a member of an affiliated organisation from another country) to stay in their many hostels round Scotland. Phone 01786 451181 for details, or contact any YHA hostel.

24
B2

✠ **SY HOSTEL:** 332 3004. 7 Park Terr. Close to where the old Glas hostel used to be in Woodlands Terr, in the same area of the W End nr the univ and Kelvingrove Park. This building was converted in 1992 from the Beacons Hotel, which was where rock 'n' roll bands used to stay in the 1980s. Now the bedrms are converted into dorms for 4-6 (some larger) and the public rms are common rms with TV, games, café, etc. Still feels more like a hotel than a hostel and is a gr place to stay. Late opening. You must be a member of the YHA. Phone for info.   99RMS

25
C3

✠ **BAIRD HALL, STRATHCLYDE UNIV:** 332 6415. 460 Sauchiehall St. The landmark Grade A-listed Art Deco building near the Art School and the W End. Originally the Beresford Hotel, built 1937 and once Glasgow's finest (v Miami Beach). 194 rms in vacs and 11 available AYR. Spartan, almost drab, though the rms are fine, like an American Y. Reeks of nostalgia as well as disinfectant. Diningrm, TV and reading rm. Lots of groovy places nearby such as Nico's, Variety Bar, Baby Grand and the Griffin. All are listed further on.   54RMS

26
D4

CLYDE HALL, STRATHCLYDE UNIV: 221 1219. 318 Clyde St. A v central block, off-campus at the bottom of Union/Renfield St and almost o/looking the river. 165 single and twin rms, mainly in summer vac. Refectory and TV rm. Some smaller rms on lower floor are available cheaply as self-catering specifically for backpackers, and are a v good deal.   30RMS

27
E3

MURRAY HALL, STRATHCLYDE UNIV: 552 4400 (ext 3560). Collins St. Modern, but not sterile block of single rms on edge of main campus and facing towards Cathedral. Part of large complex (also some student flats to rent by the week) with bar/shop/laundrette. Quite central, close to Merchant City bars. Vacs only.   134RMS

28
xB1

QUEEN MARGARET HALL, GLASGOW UNIV: 334 2192. 55 Bellshaugh Rd. Off-campus (in fact, rather a long way from anything) but a big high-rise block of comfortable rms where there's a good chance of accom when more central halls are full. Get a bike. Vacs only.   134RMS

CAIRNCROSS HOUSE, GLASGOW UNIV: 330 5385. Kelvinhaugh Pl, off Argyle St at Murphy's Pakora Bar. Nr Kelvingrove Park, Byres Rd and some good pubs and Indian restaus, a recently-built student-hall complex not brickful of ambience, but well appointed and convenient. Vacs only.

29
A2

Note: Both Strathclyde and Glasgow Universities have several halls of residence available for short-term accom in the summer months. For those above (the best of them) and others, you may also phone: Glasgow 330 5385 or Strathclyde 553 4148 (central booking)

THE BEST CAMPING AND CARAVAN PARKS

Refer to Around Glasgow Map on pages 118–19.

30
E3

STRATHCLYDE PARK: 01698 266155. 20km SE of Glas. M74 at jnct 6 or M8/A725. On the edge of a large popular country park and easily reached by the motorway system. Go left just after park entrance. Check in until 9.30pm. Stay up to 2 weeks. Usual but good standard facs on site and many others nearby, e.g. café, windsurfing, gym till 8.30pm, 500m away. Motorway close, so traffic noise, but no visual intrusion on this well-managed parkland site. Caravans and tents separate. Glasgow's most accessible caravan park by car. 150 pitches. Apr-Oct. (387/403/OUTSIDE GLASGOW)

31
C3

BARNBROCK, LOCHWINNOCH: 01505 614791. 40km SW of Glas via M8/A8 Pt Glas then Kilmacolm rd A761, then B786; or via Johnstone on A737, A760 to Lochwinnoch. Let's face it, it's not exactly convenient, but this beautiful, remote site (camping only) is on the edge of the wild and wonderful Muirshiel Country Park and Lochwinnoch Nature Reserve and it's not far to go to leave the city behind completely. 15 tents. (388/OUTSIDE GLASGOW)

32
C3

CLOCH CARAVAN PARK, GOUROCK: 01475 632675. 45km W of Glas along the coast. Take M8 then A8 through Greenock and Gourock; continue for 6km. Residential caravan park (no tents) with only a few touring pitches. Best feature is that it o/looks the historical Cloch Pt Lighthouse and the R Clyde. 10 places only.

33
D2

TULLICHEWAN, BALLOCH: 01389 759475. 40km NW of Glas. A fair distance from the city, but fast rds in this direction via A82 (dual carriageway all the way), or via Erskine Br and then M8. Best to leave the car here and take frequent train service from Balloch Stn nearby; 30mins to Glas Central Stn. This park is nicely situated nr L Lomond and tourist centres and is well managed and good fun for kids. Shop, laundrette, games rm, TV, sauna, sunbeds, etc. Probably the best park for holiday-making hereabouts. 140 places.

34
C2

ARDLUI, LOCH LOMOND: 01301 704243. Continue on A82 (from above). At the other end of the loch in an ideal spot for exploring by boat (they have hiring facs and a 100 berth marina) or on foot. For self-catering, 6-8 berth caravans are available and there's an on-site hotel (11 rms, 2 bars and 2 restaus) if your tent blows away in the night. Laundry, children's play area, shop. 97 places.

22

THE BEST HOTELS OUTSIDE TOWN

Refer to Around Glasgow Map on pages 118–19.

✠ GLEDDOCH HOUSE, LANGBANK, nr GREENOCK: 01475 540711.
Take the M8/A8 to Greenock, then the B789 signposted
Langbank/Houston, then 2km – hotel is signed. 30km W of centre by fast rd. A château-like country-house hotel, formerly the
home of the Lithgow Shipping family. High above the Clyde estu-
ary, there are spectacular views across to Dumbarton Rock and the
Kilpatrick Hills. Rms not lavish but comfortable, only a few have
the view. Reputable dining-rm strong on Scottish ingredients and
cuisine. Pleasant conservatory. Excellent 18-hole golf course
(294/SPORTS FACILITIES); health club, tiny pool.

35
C3

37RMS JAN-DEC T/T PETS CC KIDS TOS LOTS

✠ CAMERON HOUSE, nr BALLOCH, LOCH LOMOND: 01389 755565.
A82 dual carriageway into W End or via Erskine Br and M8.
45km NW of centre. Highly regarded mansion-house hotel complex with excellent leisure facs in open grounds on the bonny banks
of the loch. Sports incl 9-hole golf, good pool, tennis and a busy
marina for sailing/windsurfing, etc. Notable restau (The Georgian
Rm) and all-day brasserie. Many famous names from Gazza to
Pavarotti have holed up here (but they wouldn't have Oasis).

36
D2

68RMS JAN-DEC T/T XPETS CC KIDS TOS LOTS

✠ THE BLACK BULL HOTEL, KILLEARN: 01360 550215. 2 The Sq.
A81 towards Aberfoyle, take the rt fork after Glengoyne
Distillery, and the hotel is at the top end of the village next to the
church. Recent change of hands; extensively refurbed, this old
hotel has been given a new lease of life. Open-plan bar/restau with
good food, spacious conservatory with enclosed grd and tastefully decorated, comfortable rms. (406/OUTSIDE GLASGOW)

37
D2

11RMS JAN-DEC T/T PETS CC KIDS MED.EXP

✠ COUNTRY CLUB HOTEL, STRATHBLANE 01360 770491. 20km N
and only 20mins from Maryhill Rd on a good day (follow
A81, the Milngavie rd, to Strathblane). Not new (refurb '97), but
inserted at time of going to press because we didn't know of it
before (no item number). A v civilised lodging to N of city with
excellent restau and more informal brasserie. Rms individual and
well appointed; good pictures.

D3

10RMS JAN-DEC T/T PETS CC KIDS EXP

38
D3
BOWFIELD COUNTRY CLUB, HOWWOOD: 01505 705225. Jnct 29 off M8 for Howwood, then 3km from Main St via steep Z-bend. 32km SW of centre. Farmhouse-like retreat in gentle hill country just beyond the conurbation. Rms in modern annex are comfortable and, with the club facs (squash, gym, saunas, etc.) and a large pool (open until 10pm), represent good value. Less earnest than usual health clubs. 23RMS JAN-DEC T/T XPETS CC KIDS EXP

39
D3
BOTHWELL BRIDGE HOTEL, BOTHWELL: 01698 852246. Uddingston t/off from M74 15km SE of centre. Main St. Nr castle (380/OUT-SIDE GLASGOW) and pub (204/'UNSPOILT' PUBS). Comfortable, family-run hotel with an Italian ambience. V kid-friendly.
75RMS JAN-DEC T/T XPETS CC KIDS EXP

40
D2
CULCREUCH CASTLE HOTEL, FINTRY: 01360 860228. Off B818 in Campsie Fells, 32km N of centre via A81 Milngavie rd from Glas. Fintry is well kept and in a valley betw the Fells and the Fintry Hills. Some fine walking (365/WALKS OUTSIDE THE CITY). Ancestral home of the Galbraiths with many old features, incl a half-tester bed. Dungeons converted into bar/bistro. Many weddings, so check w/ends. 8RMS JAN-DEC T/T PETS CC KIDS TOS MED.INX

41
D2
THE BALLOCH HOTEL, BALLOCH, LOCH LOMOND: 01389 752579. 40km NW of centre by fast rds (*see* Cameron House *above*) or frequent and convenient train. Busy hotel (beer grd and local bar) in a tourist centre by lochside moorings. It goes like the Glas Fair in the summer. 14RMS JAN-DEC T/T PETS CC KIDS MED.INX

42
C3
THE INVERKIP HOTEL, INVERKIP: 01475 521478. M8 from Glas then A8 and A78 from Pt Glas heading S for Largs. 50km W of centre. Inverkip is a wee bypassed village now dominated from the other side of the main rd by the Kip Marina (401/OUTSIDE GLASGOW). Hotel is in Main St; a family-run coaching inn with busy pub downstairs. The most reasonable place to stay on this part of the Clyde coast. 5RMS JAN-DEC X/T PETS CC KIDS INX

43
C3
KIRKTON HOUSE, CARDROSS: 01389 841951. Darleith Rd. A814, past Helensburgh to Cardross village then N up Darleith Rd. Kirkton House is 1km on rt. 18th-century Scottish farmhouse that combines rustic charm with *every* mod con (check your web site). Informal and unpretentious ('no hang-ups'), quality home-cooking and a stone's throw from L Lomond. International clientele.
6 RMS JAN-DEC T/T PETS CC KIDS MED.INX

BAIRD HALL 'landmark Grade A-listed Art Deco building' (page 20)

Alfresco dining at the Italian Centre in the
Merchant City

WHERE TO EAT

YES 'currently the best restaurant in town'
(page 29)

THE BEST RESTAURANTS

✝ ✝ **YES:** 221 8044. 22 W Nile St. Downtown and downstairs (though street-level café-bar is a good place to meet and the 'Brasserie Menu' one of the best-value light meals in town) is the airy and uncluttered creation of Ferrier Richardson and currently the best restau in town. Poss down to chef Iain MacMaster who in the last edition of this book was at the Puppet Theatre (*see below*). Some Asian/Pacific influence to superbly balanced dishes presented with flair and no fuss. Lunch and LO 11pm (upstairs 9pm). Both cl Sun.   MED

44
D3

✝ ✝ **THE BUTTERY:** 221 8188. 652 Argyle St. Central but curious location for Glasgow's most consistently superb restau owned, as is the Rogano (*see below*), by Alloa Breweries. Occupying the only remaining tenement block in an area carved up by urban developers, the Buttery and its little brother downstairs, the Belfry (66/BEST BISTROS), are best reached via the westerly extension of St Vincent St then Elderslie St. New chef Willie Deans, kent face of the Scottish culinary Olympic team, pepping up the menu but comfortable old-fashioned ambience remains. No changes should depose the winning sample-all-desserts option. 6 days lunch and 7-10pm. Cl Sun and Sat lunch.   EXP

45
B3

✝ ✝ **NAIRN'S:** 353 0707. 13 Woodside Cres, nr Charing Cross (and Thai Fountain – *see below*). Ubiquitous telly chef Nick Nairn's highly anticipated newish restau (late '97) on 2 floors in this W End town house (accom in 4 rms upstairs – see 4/BEST HOTELS). Still settling in at time of going to press, but hits all the right spots in urban contemporary dining – smart, confident cuisine and service. You'd be hard put to find anywhere else of this quality at these prices.   MED

46
B2

✝ **PUPPET THEATRE:** 339 8444. 11 Ruthven Lane. In a converted mews behind Byres Rd, one of Scotland's most stylish restaus. Intimate dining areas; the crescent-shaped conservatory is the most popular and may be tightly packed. Fixed-price menus. Contemporary British with Scottish slant and impeccable ingredients and presentation. Lunch (not Sat); LO 11pm. Cl Mon.   EXP

47
A1

✝ **ROGANO:** 248 4055. 11 Exchange Pl. Betw Buchanan St and Queen St. An institution in Glas since the 1930s. Décor replicating a Cunard ship, the *Queen Mary,* is the major attraction. It's *the* place to take visiting friends or meet clients, even if just for cocktails. The restau is spacious and perennially fashionable, with

48
D4

fish and seafood the specialities. Downstairs, the supper and 'luncheon rm has a lighter/cheaper menu, and though it's a bit sub-Rogano its informality is easier on the pocket. Restaurant: lunch and 6-10.30pm. Café Rogano: lunch and 6-11pm (Fri-Sat until 12midnight, Sun until 10pm).   EXP.MED

49
xB1

✢ **ONE DEVONSHIRE GARDENS:** 339 2001. Glasgow's most stylish hotel (1/BEST HOTELS) has a restau which has won accolades in its own rt. Like the sumptuous surroundings, dishes on the fixed-price menu are contemporary, voguish and seductive. Staff are young and friendly. All in all, a food experience that doesn't feel like you're in a hotel.   EXP

50
A1

✢ **THE UBIQUITOUS CHIP:** 334 5007. 12 Ashton Lane. A corner-stone of Glasgow's culinary establishments. Two-storey, covered courtyard draped with vines, off a cobbled lane in the heart of the W End, heaped with accolades over 26yrs in residence. The main bit is still one of the most atmospheric of rms. The menu is based on exemplary fresh Scottish seafood, the best of game and beef and fine, original cooking. All complemented by an outstanding wine list. Daily lunch and 6.30-11pm. (69/BEST BISTROS)   EXP

51
xA2

✢ **THE CABIN:** 569 1036. 996 Dumbarton Rd. New chef David Dempsie joins Denis Dwyer's capable team in the kitchen, and, if anything, it's even better than before. Beautifully cooked fresh seafood and Scottish game, home-made Irish soda bread and delicious puds. You'll probably have to linger after dinner, when Wilma, legendary waitress and *chanteuse,* does her diva thing. Unique. BYOB. Tue-Sat lunch and 7.30-9.30pm. LO 9pm.   MED

52
°*B1*

✢ **STRAVAIGIN:** 334 2665. 28 Gibson St. 50m downhill from Glas Univ's Men's Union, that is to say, in the v heart of bohemia, is where you'll find this underground restau. Stravaigin has a constantly changing menu, with a range and diversity that is truly eclectic, mixing international cuisines, esp Asian and Pacific Rim, to an effect that Asian restaus themselves rarely achieve. Fresh ideas and the freshest of ingredients combine to put this restau in a class of its own. Herald Chef of the Year 1998. Mon-Thu 12noon-12midnight, Fri-Sat 12noon-1am, Sun 5pm-12midnight. INX

53
A2

✢ **TWO FAT LADIES:** 339 1944. 88 Dumbarton Rd, along from Kelvingrove Museum nr the end of Byres Rd. Calum

Mathieson's seafood bistro is not just any old pt in a storm; in Glas it's about the only pt in a storm if you want first-class seafood. Easy on the eye and palate (nothing too fancy) and for this integrity and reliability, easy on the pocket. Simply sound. Tues-Sat LO 10pm, lunch Fri-Sat only. Cl Sun. (124/SEAFOOD RESTAUS)   MED

✚ **THAI FOUNTAIN:** 332 2599. 2 Woodside Cres, Charing Cross. Same ownership as Amber Regent (*see below*), this is probably Glasgow's best Asian restau. Genuinely Thai and not at all Chinese. Innovative dishes with gr diversity of flavours and textures, so sharing several is best. Of course you will eat too much. Cl Sun. (101/FAR-EASTERN RESTAUS)   MED

54
B2

✚ **LA PARMIGIANA:** 334 0686. 447 Gr Western Rd. Simply the best Italian for many (convenient location nr Kelvin Br – usually parking nearby), the favourite place to eat without the ceremony and dulcet tones. Contemporary, perhaps predictable, cuisine. For when you can't face anything that isn't lightly done in olive oil. LO 11pm. Cl Sun. (73/ITALIAN RESTAUS)   MED

55
B1

✚ **BOUZY ROUGE:** 221 8804. 111 W Regent St. Sister retau of the Bouzy Rouge in Airdrie (01236 763853), this is an excellent unpretentious downtown bistro. Owned by the Brown family, with chef Paul Holmes it repeats the Airdrie formula of eclectic, affordable contemporary food and wine. Gr for breakfast and Sun lunch. 7 days, 9.30am-12midnight. Sun 12noon-12midnight. LO 10pm. Popular; booking may be necessary.   INX

56
C3

GINGERHILL: 956 6515. Hillhead St, Milngavie. At the end of the pedestrianised centre of Milngavie (15km N of centre), an intimate, friendly upstairs parlour. Restau specialising in seafood with excellent fresh produce (Gigha-landed fish, etc.). Mon-Sat 11am-4pm. Thu-Sat 7pm onwards. (125/SEAFOOD RESTAUS)   INX

57
xC1

BUDDA: 243 2212. 142 St Vincent St. Downstairs bar with N African slant and this up-and-coming restau behind the drapes at the back. Too new at time of going to press to give more than a mention, but expect to hear more from chef Rachel McTavish. Mon-Sat lunch and LO 10.30pm. Sun dinner only.   INX

58
D3

AMBER REGENT: 50 West Regent St. Report: 102/FAR-EASTERN.

KILLERMONT POLO CLUB: 2002 Maryhill Rd. Report: 92/INDIAN.

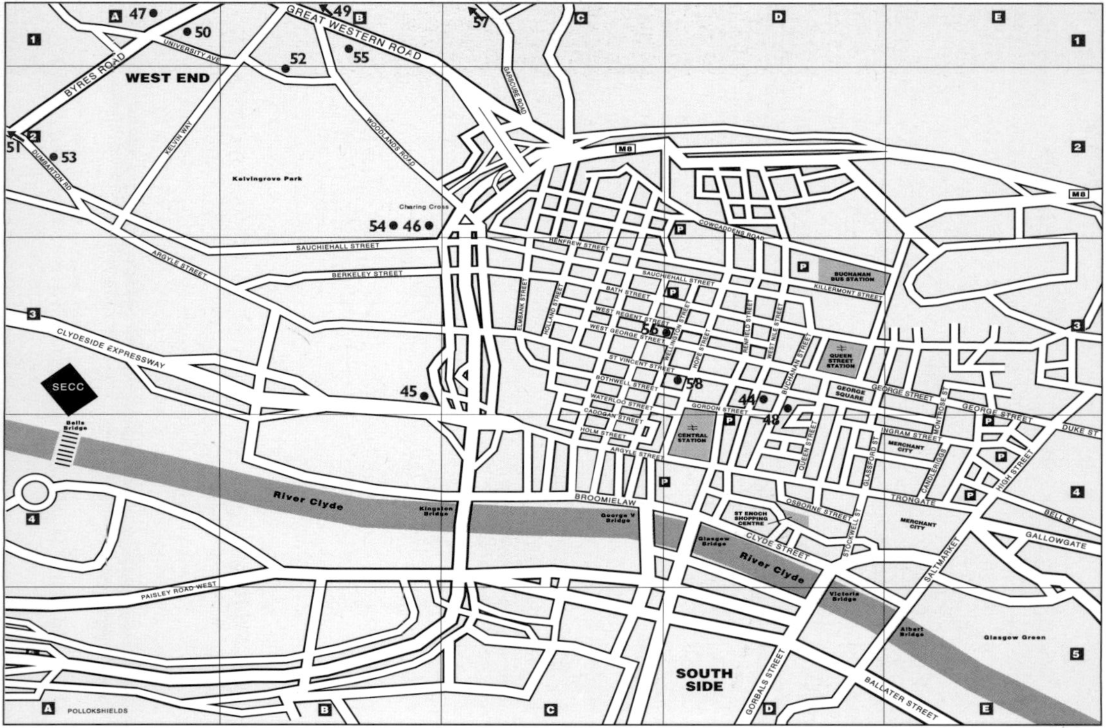

WEST END

SOUTH SIDE

Kelvingrove Park

Glasgow Green

River Clyde

River Clyde

SECC

POLLOKSHIELDS

GREAT WESTERN ROAD

BYRES ROAD

DUMBARTON ROAD

SAUCHIEHALL STREET

ARGYLE STREET

CLYDESIDE EXPRESSWAY

PAISLEY ROAD WEST

GARSCUBE ROAD

Charing Cross

BUCHANAN BUS STATION

QUEEN STREET STATION

CENTRAL STATION

George Square

ST ENOCH SHOPPING CENTRE

BROOMIELAW

GORBALS STREET

BALLATER STREET

GALLOWGATE

47
50
52
55
49
57
54 46
45
56
58
44 48
51 53

STRAVAIGIN 'a range and diversity that is truly eclectic' (page 30)

THE BEST BISTROS AND CAFÉ-BARS

59
B3, A1

✚ **MITCHELLS:** 204 4312. 2 branches, both W. 157 N St on the left bank of the M8 at the Mitchell Library, next to the Bon Accord (212/REAL-ALE PUBS). Ales here too, but notably *the* place for informal and v good food with a genuine bistro atmos. Intimate, more colourful version in busy Ashton Lane off Byres Rd (339 2220) has helpful BYOB, inexp pre-theatre menu and more laid-back atmos. Both have food until 11pm, bar until 12midnight. Cl Sun.   INX

60
C3

✚ **MALMAISON:** 221 6401. 278 W George St. The brasserie in the basement of the hotel (2/BEST HOTELS) with the same setup in Edin and a v similar menu. Excellent brasserie ambience in meticulously designed woody salon. Seating layout and busy waiters mean lots of buzz; also private dining-rms and the adjacent **CAFÉ MAL** in bright contrast. Fixed-menu lunch or dinner Mediterranean style with daily specials. 7 days, lunch and LO 10.30pm.   MED

61
D3

✚ **PAPINGO:** 332 6678. 104 Bath St. Bright bistro in a cool basement with an accomplished new chef and a fresh outlook. The food is Scottish/French and perfectly portioned, especially for pre-theatre dinner. Wines and waiters are esp well chosen. Daily until 10.30/11pm.   INX

62
C3

✚ **MOJO:** 331 2257. 158a Bath St. Discreet, comfortable bistro behind the curtains at the back of this busy, metropolitan basement bar. The menu features some Japanese dishes such as sushi/sashimi, which are just as confidently produced as the more trad steak/frites. Relaxed atmos; straight-talking wine list. But it's mainly down to the chef, John Quigley, and at the time of going to press he was maybe moving. If you're a foodie, do check first. Mon-Sat 12noon-12midnight, Sun 6pm-12midnight. (238/THESE ARE HIP)   INX

63
C3

✚ **BABY GRAND:** 248 4942. 3-7 Elmbank Grds. Inviting haven among high-rise office blocks opp Charing Cross Tower Hotel (13/INEXPENSIVE HOTELS); a downtown-USA location. (Go behind the King's Theatre down Elmbank St, rt at gas stn and look for the hotel.) Probably the best urban atmos on this page. Narrow rm with bar stools and banquettes, often with background music from the eponymous piano. Light, eclectic menu from tapas to full meals materialise in the tiny gantry. Daily from 8am-12midnight/1am. We'll say it again (they *did* like it), 'Only real cities have places like this.'   CHP

COTTIER'S: 357 5827. 93 Hyndland Rd. Off the top of Hyndland St nr Highburgh Rd. Converted church that encompasses a bar; regular live music (254/LIVE MUSIC) and benches o/side, a restau with an interesting menu made up of light, spicy dishes mostly from S of the Mason-Dixon line, and a theatre that stages a broad range of productions/music throughout the yr. An autonomous state really (probably have their own football team). (180/SUNDAY BREAKFAST and many other reasons.) 7 days.   INX

64
xA1

BLUE BANANA: 959 2722. 42 Munro Pl. Through Anniesland Cross, going W on Gr Western Rd. Turn into first Esso garage on left (really!) and it's through the gateway on the left. Madeleine Valente's friendly, 'family kitchen'-style bistro. A variety of Scottish/international dishes, combining the freshest of ingredients and the cooking expertise of her extended family. Mon-Sat lunch and 6-11pm.   MED

65
xB1

THE BELFRY: 221 0630. 652 Argyle St. App via W extension of St Vincent St, Elderslie St and left at the conical church. The basement of the Buttery, one of Glasgow's finest restaus (45/BEST RESTAUS), in the one remaining tenement of an area savaged by the M8. Bistro version of the Scots/French cuisine served up top, in study-like cellar rms with dark wood and books. New star chef so eat the best for less. Mon-Sat lunch, 6-11pm. Cl Sun.   INX

66
B3

CUL DE SAC: 334 8899. 44 Ashton Lane, the main lane off Byres Rd with the Grosvenor Cinema and The Ubiquitous Chip (50/BEST RESTAUS). Perennially fashionable crêperie/ diner dedicated to serving good, simple food with flair, even wit. The atmos is relaxed and conversational, the burgers are exceptional and the fresh exotic flowers add a final *touché* (181/SUNDAY BREAKFAST). Daily 12noon-11pm (Fri-Sat 12midnight).   CHP

67
A1

BAR BREL: 342 4966. 39 Ashton Lane. The unstoppable Billy McAnnanie's latest wheeze – a Gallic bar/bistro across the lane from the Cul de Sac (*see above*). Flagstone floor, metal tables and enormous folding doors. No mistaking the Belgian influence in the cooking; fat, crispy chips served with large bowls of steaming mussels, or with steak. No Belgian jokes, but Belgian beers and a good wine list. Daily 11am-11pm (Fri-Sat until 12midnight).   INX

68
A1

69
A1

UPSTAIRS AT THE CHIP: 334 5007. 12 Ashton Lane. At other end of lane from Cul de Sac (*see above*) and upstairs from The Ubiquitous Chip (50/BEST RESTAUS), this is the wine bar and cheap seats version of the celebrated restau. Some tables are around the gallery of the courtyard below. There's a different menu with some similar seafood and puds, as well as bar-type salads and soups, etc. The bill will be less and you still get the celebrated wine list. Lively atmos. (183/SUNDAY BREAKFAST)   INX

70
E4

TRON CAFÉ-BAR: 552 8587. 63 Trongate. Attached to the important Tron Theatre (327/NIGHTLIFE), presently undergoing a major face-lift. The buzzing bar/bistro at the back has New Glas clientele, decent house wines and an eclectic menu. Not always the best grub in the city, but definitely up there for atmos and generally good vibes. Food until 10.30/11pm. Cl Mon evening.   CHP

71
E4

BARGO: 553 4771. 80 Albion St. Huge, Merchant City bar and bistro in demand for fashion shoots due to its lofty stylish design. Big windows though not much to watch. The menu is a bit of a contemporary mix and match, but ain't bad considering this is more of a bar to be seen in (dreaming of Manhattan). Popular pre-club venue (233/THESE ARE HIP) but often weirdly quiet midweek. 7 days, 10am-12midnight. LO for food 10pm.   INX

THE BEST ITALIAN RESTAURANTS

✠ ✠ **FRATELLI SARTI:** 248 2228, 133 Wellington St, and 204 0440 (best number for bookings), 121 Bath St. Glasgow's famed *emporio d'Italia* combining a deli in Wellington St, wine shop in Bath St and restaus in each. Gr bustling atmos. Cultivated and celebrated by anyone who has ever managed to get a table at lunchtime. Good pizza, specials change every day, *dolci* and *gelati* in super-calorific abundance. LO 10.30pm. Cl Sun. (87/PIZZA, 162/COFFEE)   CHP

72
D3

✠ **LA PARMIGIANA:** 334 0686. 447 Gr Western Rd. Sophisticated ristorante that blends trad service and contemporary Italian cuisine into one seamless performance. Carefully chosen dishes and wine list; solicitous service. Milano rather than Napoli. Expect to find Italians (who consider this to be one of the city's gr restaus – 55/BEST RESTAUS). Mon-Sat lunch and 6-11pm. Cl Sun.   MED

73
B1

✠ **LA FIORENTINA:** 420 1585. 2 Paisley Rd W. Not far from river and motorway over Kingston Br, but app from Eglinton St (A77 Kilmarnock Rd). It's at the Y-jnct with Govan Rd. Trad tratt in an imposing listed building with an angel on top. Always busy, usually seafood specials and off-hand waiters who break into the occasional aria. As Italian as you want it to be, gr atmos with enormous menu and wine list. Mon-Sat lunch and 5.30-11pm (though LO 9.30pm). Cl Sun.   MED

74
B4

MASSIMO: 332 3227. 57 Elmbank St. Downstairs and across the st from King's Theatre. Family-run café/bar/ristorante where they joke about our lengthy 'rainy season' and serve good pasta/pizza with a 'sunny' attitude. 6 days 9.30-11.30, cl Sun.   INX

75
C3

SAL E PEPE: 341 0999. 18 Gibson St. By the same people who run the Di Maggio's chain of kid-friendly eateries (137/KID-FRIENDLY), a split-level tratt that's a departure from the spag 'n' rag formula. This a tad Tuscan, somewhat sun-dried tomato but nice moist meatloaf and v crispy pizza (89/PIZZA). Puds poor; *caffè latte* a better bet than just *gelati*. A Sun brunch fave. 7 days.   MED

76
B1

RISTORANTE CAPRESE: 332 3070. 217 Buchanan St. Basement café nr the Concert Hall. Glaswegians (and footballers) love this place judging by the rogues' gallery of happy smiling punters. Checked tablecloths and Dino crooning in the background create the authentic 'mamma mia' atmos. Friendly service, constantly mobbed (well, not *mobbed*). LO 10/11pm. Book at w/ends.   INX

77
D3

78
C3

PAPERINO'S: 332 3800. 283 Sauchiehall St. Of course when you look into the good Glas restaus of a type, you find they're often owned by the same people. That explains why this ordinary-looking though quite smart restau is better than the rest – it's the same family as La Parmigiana (*see above*) and The Big Blue (227/PUB FOOD). Pasta and pizza here are always just fine. 7 days. LO 11pm/12midnight.   INX

79
C1

CAFÉ DU SUD: 332 2054. 8 Clarendon St. Recently opened, immediately popular little restau tucked away behind St George's Cross. Mediterranean/Italian-style cooking from husband-and-wife team who run it with an emphasis on the personal touch. Everything seems fresh and home-made. Better book. Mon-Sat lunch 12noon-3pm and 6-10.30pm. Cl Sun.   INX

80
D3

PIZZA EXPRESS: 221 3333. 151 Queen St, nr George Sq. The first of several, stylishly designed PEs in Scotland. Peter Boizot's finely-tuned formula translated here with moderate success. Occasional jazz and the gospel of good pizza heard every evening. Pasta, but only 2; some salads. 7 days until 11.30pm. (85/PIZZA)   INX

81
A1

ANTIPASTI: 337 2737. 337 Byres Rd. Popular restau on 2 levels that spills onto the st in warm weather, bringing a touch of *la dolce vita* to the corner of Observatory Rd. Good pasta, shame that if you just want an espresso and dessert you can't have it alfresco. Breakfast time until late (12midnight w/ends). Also at 305 Sauchiehall St (332 9002). Same food, same vibe. New but looks good. 7 days, am until late.   INX

82
B1

TREVI: 334 3262. 526 Gr Western Rd. Tiny family-run tratt with celebrity photos next to Italia league memorabilia on the walls. The staff can get a bit distracted on international fixture nights. Loyal clientele; specials change every day. Tasty home-made focaccia. Mon-Fri lunch and 6-11pm, Sat-Sun 6-11pm.   INX

83
xC5

ARIGO: 636 6616. 67 Kilmarnock Rd, Shawlands. Smart little Italian joint on busiest stretch of this main drag. Waiters in the long aprons-u-like. Spare, colour-tint décor. Some surprises on the menu, e.g. *pollo e crozzo risotto* (with mussels). Proper wines. 7 days lunch and dinner. LO 10.30pm.   INX

84
D3

FAZZI'S: 332 0941. 67 Cambridge St. Across the rd from the Glas Thistle Hotel. This once gr deli/café (and some say it's gone rt down the pasta tube) included here more for nostalgia than now.

They still like to put their more glamorous customers by the window . . . well it pays to advertise, so you might or might not get a good view of the neighbourhood, as well as a decent cappuccino. 8am-10pm, Sun 11am-9pm.   INX

THE BEST PIZZA

PIZZA EXPRESS: 221 3333. 151 Queen St. The national chain, but still the best of them. Here (nr George Sq) in an airy rm upstairs and down when it's busy. They do know how to make pizza, so this is a reliable standby, esp when your party can't agree on anywhere else. 7 days until 11.30pm. (80/ITALIAN RESTAUS)

85
D3

LITTLE ITALY: 339 6287. 205 Byres Rd. Ready-made slices and 3 sizes of superb made-to-order takeaway pies. You'll have to wait, but it's worth it. Have a coffee (164/COFFEE). Mon-Thu 8am-10pm, Fri-Sat 8am-1am, Sun 5-10pm. (189/TAKEAWAY)

86
A1

FRATELLI SARTI: 248 2228. 133 Wellington St and 121 Bath St. Excellent, thin-crust pie, buffalo mozzarella and freshly-made *pomodoro*. Open 8am-10pm. Cl Sun. Full report: 72/ITALIAN RESTAUS.

87
D3

MASSIMO: 332 3227. 57 Elmbank St. Downstairs and across the street from King's Theatre, this family-run café/bar/ristorante has good pizza; 'light as a feather' crust and they'll make up any combo you like to order. 6 days 9.30am-11.30pm. Cl Sun. (168/COFFEE)

88
C3

SAL E PEPE: 341 0999. 18 Gibson St. Nr Glas Univ, this is the newest of the new crop of Tuscan-influenced Italian bistros and part of the Di Maggio family chain (137/KID-FRIENDLY). Good thin-crust base and a chilli *pomodoro* option that makes a change for veggies. 7 days, 9.30am-11pm. (76/ITALIAN RESTAUS)

89
B1

CINE CITTÀ: 332 6789. 327 Sauchiehall St. Trad oven-baked, thin-based pizza with all the usual freshly-prepared goodies that go on top; in the nite-zone. 7 days until 11pm.

90
C3

SANNINO: 332 8025, 61 Bath St, and 332 3565, 61 Elmbank St. Famous in Glas for its enormous 16 inch pizzas, made for sharing. You can go half and half with the toppings. 7 days, 12noon-12midnight.

91
D3, C3

THE BEST INDIAN RESTAURANTS

92
xC1

✝ **KILLERMONT POLO CLUB:** 946 5412. 2022 Maryhill Rd. The more genuine traditions of the days of the Raj are still in evidence at Killermont. Within a hill-top restau, at the Milngavie end of Maryhill Rd, you will find courteous manners, attentive service and a clubby atmos in the front rm, which is kept as a shrine to all things polo (and they *do* run their own team). The food is fresh, light and the spices are sprinkled with care. Here Indian cuisine is taken seriously and they experiment in their Sun-Tue buffet-dinner. Lunch (not Sun) and 5pm-12midnight (LO 10.30pm).

MED

93
B3

✝ **MOTHER INDIA:** 221 1663. 28 Westminster Terr, nr the Kelvin Park Lorne Hotel (10/BEST HOTELS). A kitchen-style restau where 'on-the-bone', a touchstone of authentic Indian home-cooking, is used to gr effect. Tired of the old trad buffet round, they've devised a new app where you can make up your own buffet, as many dishes as you like all freshly prepared. Lots of vegn choice. V relaxed neighbourhood atmos. BYOB. 7 days lunch and LO 10.30pm.

INX

94
B3

CRÈME DE LA CRÈME: 221 3222. 1071 Argyle St. The biggest, the most flash (and god knows they love flash) restau in town – or anywhere for that matter – so *they* say. Still at the hot edge of all things curried with the intro of a newly extended Goanese-style menu. Frequently busy with office parties and leaving-dos, which keeps the place buzzing. Behind the flambé and the razzmatazz this is a restau that is run with care and, dare we say, precision. 7 days, lunch (not Sun) and LO 11pm.

MED

95
A1, B3

ASHOKA ASHTON LANE: 357 5904. 19 Ashton Lane. Front-line curry shop for students from Glasgow Univ, just up the lane. V popular, v customer-led, so the food is strong on flavour and generously portioned. Can do no wrong, some say. **ASHOKA WEST END:** 339 0936. 1284 Argyle St. Has always been a good, simple and dependable place to go for a bite of curry, but now seeming pricey to the faithful and, shock-horror, some are going elsewhere. Still, the healthy option menu is a good idea and on Sun family night, kids eat free. Both 7 days, lunch and open until 12midnight (W End even later).

INX

96
B3

MR SINGH'S INDIA: 221 1452. 149 Elderslie St. In an up-and-coming part of town this restau has acquired a reputation for consistency and kilted (really!) affability and has so far avoided the buffet trap. Simply better than most. It's perfectly placed to take on all (new)comers. 7 days, lunch and LO 11.30pm.   INX

CAFÉ INDIA: 248 4074. 171 N St. Enormous brasserie, big on a glamour that seems a bit time-warped now, but the food is pretty good and presented in a way to make *you* feel good too. (*Group hug.*) The extensive menu is busy with herbs and spices and is not merely hot. A night on the town kind of joint. Buffet Sun-Mon. 7 days, lunch and LO 11.30pm/12midnight.   INX

97
B3

SHISH MAHAL: 334 1057. 68 Park Rd. First-generation Indian restau that still, after 30yrs, remains one of Glasgow's faves rather than finest. Though it's been a long time since Billy Connolly immortalized the vindaloo here, faithful followers swear it's yet to be bettered. But changes afoot. Until 11pm/12midnight.   INX

98
B2

KAMA SUTRA: 332 0055. 331 Sauchiehall St. Part of the Ashoka group, this new restau has built a reputation for good food. An extensive and adventurous menu where each dish comes with a breakdown of contents and region of origin. Extracts from the original Indian sex-guide dotted here and there are peered at, surreptitiously. Those positions may put you off your dinner – never mind the pointy bits. 7 days, lunch and until 12midnight (Fri-Sat until 1am).   INX

99
C3

THE ASHOKA: 221 1761. 108 Elderslie St. Confusingly, no relation to those above. Designery interior but that old pink pakora sauce still runs through the veins. Recently voted No. 1 in the 'Best curry houses in Scotland' – that's a matter of taste but it is hot (and hot). Mon-Sat lunch, 7 days dinner. LO 11.30pm.   INX

100
B3

THE BEST FAR-EASTERN RESTAURANTS

101
B2

✝ **THAI FOUNTAIN:** 332 2599. 2 Woodside Cres. Charing Cross, nr the motorway, Mitchell Library, etc. Few Thai restaus in Glas; this one clearly the best (and probably the best in Scotland). Owned by Chinese Mr Chung (*see* Amber Regent, *below*), but the Thai chefs know a green curry from a red. Tom yam excellent and weeping tiger beef v popular with those who really just want a steak. Lots of prawn and fish dishes and real vegn choice. Lunch and LO 11pm. Cl Sun. MED

102
D3

✝ **AMBER REGENT:** 331 1655. 50 W Regent St. Elegant Cantonese restau that prides itself on courteous service and the quality of its food. The menu is trad with dishes designed to be eaten using chopsticks, although cutlery, of course, is provided. Candle-lit booths, sumptuous décor and a creditable wine list. Quite romantic, and just about always in the *Michelin* guide. Lunch, LO 11pm (Fri 11.30pm, Sat 12midnight). Cl Sun. MED

103
D4

HO WONG: 221 3550. 82 York St, in city centre nr river, betw Clyde St and Argyle St. Discreet, urbane Pekingese/Cantonese restau which relies on its reputation and makes few compromises. Décor dated now, but still up-market clientele; roomful of suits at lunch and Bolly, Moët and DP on the champagne list. Notable for seafood and duck. Best Szechuan in town (you cool down with a sorbet). Lunch (not Sun) and LO 11.30pm. MED

104
D3

PEKING INN: 332 8971. 191 Hope St. The revolving hot-plate/server at the centre of the table was an innovation when first introduced here. Since then there has been many a slip 'twixt cup and lip in the course of lengthy, exploratory meals fuelled by endless jugs of hot saki. Famous for its spicy, Szechuan specials; and good times. Lunch and LO 11.15pm (w/ends 12.15am). MED

105
C3

LOON FUNG: 332 1240. 417 Sauchiehall St. One of Glasgow's most respected Cantonese restaurants. Traditionally the place where the local Chinese community meet for lunch with their families and on a Sun/Mon/Tue, the pace is fast and friendly while the food, as you would expect, is fresh and authentic. Everybody on chopsticks. 7 days, 12noon-10/11pm. MED

106
C3

THE NOODLE BAR: 333 1883. 482 Sauchiehall St. Authentic, Chinese-style noodle bar, 100m from Charing Cross. Choose one of the 4 types of rice or egg noodles as a base, then decide whether you would like it prepared as a soup (yes, you would), add some meat or veg from the menu board, take a ticket and while you're translating the 'chinese script only' specials, your food will arrive. Truly groovy. 7days, 12noon-5am. (173/LATE-NIGHT RESTAUS)

CHP

AMBER RESTAURANT: 339 6121. 130 Byres Rd. Trad Chinese restau with an informal attitude and helpful staff. Recently extended selection of vegn dishes. V popular takeaway/home-delivery service; their chow mein is the best in the W End. Lunch except Sat-Sun and 5-11.30pm.

107
A1

INX

PATTAYA: 572 0071. 473 Sauchiehall St. A recent, and welcome, addition to the cadre. The ambience is cool and calming, a long way from Bangkok. And any holidays in Pattaya are probably best forgotten. Lengthy menu requires 2 beers-worth of perusal to do it justice. All the old lemon grass favourites are available and some thought has gone into creating authentic vegn alternatives. Mon-Fri lunch and 5.30-11.30pm, Sat-Sun until 12midnight.

108
C3

MED

MATA HARI: 332 9789. 17 W Princes St. Malaysian and Singaporean cuisine which is halal. Less spicy than Thai, with the exotic flavours of star flower and fresh cinnamon present along with the more usual lemon grass and ginger. There are some meat dishes but the menu is split mainly between vegn and seafood, with an authentic street-vendor's noodle dish that's straight off Clarke Quay, Singapore. 7 days, 5-11pm, Fri-Sat until 11.30pm.

109
B1

INX

THE BEST MEXICAN RESTAURANTS

Glas has innumerable restaus and café-bars with Mexican choices on a menu that mixes food from all over (best to stick to the potato skins). The places below are best Mex:

110
E4

PANCHO VILLAS: 552 7737. 26 Bell St. Bright, colourful restau free of the cluttered cantina stereotype, run by real, live Mexican, Maira Nunez. Menu in Spanish/ingredients in English. No burritos ('an American invention'). Plenty of veggie choices but you really have to try the *albondigas en salsa* (that's spicy meatballs). Mon-Sat lunch and 6-11pm, Sun until 10pm.   INX

111
D4

CANTINA DEL REY: 552 4044. 6 King's Court in E End nr St Enoch's glasshouse. Frozen margaritas a must in this spacious bar/restau which actually does feel like a cantina. Fajitas (with floury tortillas and spicy dips) a favourite among the *comidas* (which also includes blackened fish) and brought sizzling across the rm to your table. Free nachos; you keep on drinking. 7 days, 12noon until LO 10pm (Fri-Sat until 11pm).   INX

112
xA2

SALSA: 337 1416. 184 Dumbarton Rd. Western off-shoot of the Cantina (*see above*), smaller, more neighbourhood-friendly. Spicy salsas of the title and all the things they accompany. As with all Mexican places, food can vary with the chef, most of whom have never been N, never mind S, of the Rio Grande, but here it's more conscientious than most. Good vegn choice. 7 days, 12noon-10pm (Fri 11pm).   INX

113
D3

TEX MEX: 332 8338. 198 Bath St. Western extension of original in Edin and every bit as slammin'. More Tex than Mex, though chicken-fried steak notable by its absence, and howzabout some corn bread while we're at it. Adj Sublime Bar (good name!) goes a bit Alamo at the w/end. 7 days, lunch and dinner. LO 10-11pm.   INX

THE BEST RESTAURANTS FROM AROUND THE WORLD

ATHENA TAVERNA: 424 0858. 778 Pollokshaws Rd. On the S Side about 2km from the river. A Greek Cypriot restau and, adj, a wine bar that's big on real ale (220/REAL-ALE PUBS). Usual klefticos, etc., chicken dishes, rabbit, feta and olives, plus the salads you get sick of on holiday then hanker after when you get home. Main courses cheap; vegn options. Indifferent wine list, but there's always the Furstenberg. Mon-Sat lunch; LO vary 10pm-1am. Cl Sun.   INX

114
xC5

CAFÉ SERGHEI: 429 1547. 67 Br St, just over the Jamaica St (or Glas) Br. Greek island evenings on a bleak rd heading S, a restau in an interesting conversion of former bank with upstairs balcony beneath impressive cupola; tiles and woodwork. Friendly, talkative waiters advise and dispense excellent Greek grub, incl vegn dishes. Better moussaka than you've had on your holidays. Fri is Greek dancing night. Lunch (not Sun) and 6-11pm, 7 days.   INX

115
D4

MISKA: 334 0594. 1321 Argyle St. Out to the W End of town, near the Art Galleries. Hugely popular Austrian/Tuscan/Slovenian restau with a bewildering choice of dishes on offer; best to order one of the set menus, sit back and enjoy an Alpen Tour. Totally unpretentious; good value for money, not easily forgotten. 7 days 12.30-10.15pm, Fri/Sat till 11.15pm.   INX

116
A2

JANSSENS: 334 9682. 1355 Argyle St, opp Kelvingrove Art Gallery. Missed out in main edition of *Scotland the Best!* and a million people wrote in to complain. It's modest and informal, but a café-restau with a Dutch twist that loadsa people like. Go Dutch if you must. 7 days, from 12noon. LO 10.30pm (Sun 9pm).   INX

117
A2

JUNKANOO: 248 7102. 111 Hope St, opp Central Stn. Glasgow's original tapas bar has gone back to its Spanish roots and rt back on form. Plenty of vegn dishes and an emphasis on organic/free-range ingredients. Real Mojitos, one of the world's best, most moreish drinks (fresh mint, limes, Havana Club). 7 days, LO 11pm.   CHP

118
D3

PRINCE ARMANY'S: 420 6660. 7 Clyde Pl. Over Jamaica St Br and under railway br on rt. Glasgow's only Arabic restau. Transforms into a club after 12midnight. Food buffet-style; join in belly dancing, but only with your chops down. Tue-Fri 5pm-12midnight, w/ends until 3am. Cl Mon. (176/LATE-NIGHT RESTAUS)   CHP

119
C4

STRAVAIGIN: 334 2665. 30 Gibson St. Report: 52/BEST RESTAUS.

THE BEST FRENCH RESTAURANTS

120
D3

78 ST VINCENT: 221 7710. 78 St Vincent St. Impressive split-level rm with an enormously high ceiling and a big mural by Glas artist Donald McLeod. Stylish cuisine balancing the tried and tested with some touches of originality. Slightly formal with an atmos of discreet efficiency. Not bad wines. Lunch (not Sun) and LO 10.30pm (10.45pm Sat-Sun).   MED

121
C3

THE BRASSERIE: 248 3801. 176 W Regent St. Related to Rogano (48/BEST RESTAUS), so seafood is their forte and menu has seasonal note. Busy in evenings, but you can usually find a nook for that tête-à-tête. Here you will find a genuine steak tartare. Good wine list, especially bin-ends and halves. Mon-Fri 12noon-11pm, Sat lunch and 6-11pm. Sun, parties only.   MED

122
D3

FROGGIE'S: 572 0007. 53 W Regent St. Café/bistro with French owners and French home-cooking app. Gone a bit cajun/creole of late, but there are still a few reminders left, viz the classic Marseillaise *soupe de poisson*. Bustling brasserie atmos. Some reasonable wines and you can BYOB. Open every day, best to book at w/ends. Mon-Sat 9am-1am; Sun 5pm-12midnight. (177/LATE-NIGHT RESTAUS)   INX

123
D4, D3

PIERRE VICTOIRE: 221 7565, 91 Miller St, and 221 9130, 165 Hope St. Another 2 extensions, along the M8, of the empire that started in Edin. Hope St, the latest addition, is contained within a large, high-ceilinged room with a cupola above the axis of the 2 dining areas which illuminates their quarterly art exhibs. Add to that monthly wine nights, co-hosted by Oddbins, and you get the impression that this is a PV with a bit more flair than the rest. Run by David Murray, who also has the one in Ayr (some say all the best ones are by the seaside). Lunch and 5-10.30pm.   INX

THE BEST SEAFOOD AND FISH RESTAURANTS

✝ ✝ **TWO FAT LADIES:** 339 1944. 88 Dumbarton Rd. Informal and bright restau that's one of Glasgow's best unkept secrets. The quality and freshness of the seafood and imaginative cooking, in the hands of chef/proprietor Calum Mathieson, make this place a reliably fine prospect whether you're a fishhead or not (curiously fewer in Glas than elsewhere). Not always open on Mon (depends on the fish dunnit?), so phone. Pre-theatre menu. Sensible short wine list. We love it! Mon/Tue-Sat 6-10pm, lunch Fri-Sat. (53/BEST RESTAUS)   MED

124
A2

✝ **GINGERHILL:** 956 6515. Hillhead St, Milngavie. Upstairs at the end of the main st in this northern suburb of Glas (you are at the start of the W Highland Way), is a restau run entirely by women mostly from the island of Gigha (like much of the seafood they serve). Fixed menu and daily specials depending on what's landed. Vegn options and some chargrilled meat. One dinner sitting only, Thu-Sat (other nights if there are more than 6 of you); light lunches Mon-Sat. BYOB, no corkage. (57/BEST RESTAUS)   MED

125
xB1

THE RED SNAPPER: 357 2186. 14 Hyndland Rd. Going W on Gr Western Rd, take a left at the 2nd set of lights after Byres Rd; restau is in The Coach House Hotel, set in the Victorian terr on rt. The bright rm and wicker furniture give the feeling of sitting on someone's porch. Although there are other options on the menu, emphasis is on seafood. The early evening table d'hôte (6-7pm) is good value at less than £8 for 2 courses. Frequently changed and affordable wine list on the blackboard. 7 days. LO 10 pm.   MED

126
xB1

THE BEST VEGETARIAN RESTAURANTS

Every café-bar in town has its veggie options on the menu. However, these are the real restaus, and see below for other places with more than a token piece of crêpe.

127
E4, D4

✝ **THE 13TH NOTE:** 553 1638. 50-60 King St. Recent move for this good attitude/good vibes café-bar with occasional live music downstairs (Tues/Thu at time of going to press). Extended and big range menu from excellent vegeburgers (100% less meat than Macdonald's) to Indian and Greek dishes. All suitable for vegans. Organic booze on offer, but also normal Glas bevvy. 7 days, 12noon-12midnight. Food LO 10.30pm. Also 13th Note Club at Clyde St. (255/LIVE MUSIC)

128
B1

BAY TREE: 334 5898. 403 Gr Western Rd. Recently changed hands so no longer a feminist co-op, just an 'old-fashioned exploitative capitalist concern now' says a member of staff, in jest we hope. Fact is the place is cleaner, a lot less militant and the food is better with a wider range and some middle-eastern dishes (owners are Iranian). All is still vegan, the sole concession being a jug of milk marked 'cows'. 7 days until 9pm (Sun until 8pm). (179/SUNDAY BREAKFAST)   CHP

129
C2

VEGVILLE DINER: 333 1771. 93-97 St George's Rd, nr Charing Cross. Media-friendly restau (TV people nearby) with poster paint décor and a lively atmos. A gr deal of thought has gone towards creating a menu that is both imaginative and tempting for veggies and non-veggies alike, and with a drinks licence in the offing, the world will indeed be their oyster (mushroom). Mon 10am-7pm, Tue/Wed 10am-10pm, Thu-Sat 10am-11pm. Cl Sun.   CHP

130
B2

GRASSROOTS: 353 3278. 48 Woodlands Rd. The foremost emporium for all things organic in Glas. The range and variety of eco-friendly products, in one place, is now large enough to offer a serious alternative to that weekly trip to the supermarket. The deli-counter is the real thing, full of tasty, 'genetically un-improved' goodies, and although there's no café at press time, there should be.

131
B1

CAFÉ ALBA: 337 2282. 61 Otago St. Popular neighbourhood café with excellent, trad vegn food. Hot dishes of the day, good salads/dressings and home-made cakes, scones and slices. Hungry univ crowd, so there's not much left beyond 2.30pm. Mon-Sat 10am-5pm. (142/BEST TEAROOMS)   CHP

THE ASHA: 221 7144. Elderslie St. Intimate, vegn Indian restau with a *hunting horn* as a centrepiece! Why not! All dishes can be be made to order; your choice of sauce and chilli-ness. 3 fixed-price Thalis and a selection of starters that are moreish than most. Some wines, but a jug of lager is probably the answer here. Lunch (except Sun), and 5-11.30pm.   INX

132
B3

THE GRANARY: 226 3770. 82 Howard St, nr St Enoch Centre. Report: 141/BEST TEAROOMS.

Restaurants serving good vegn food but which are not exclusively vegn:

PUPPET THEATRE, **THE UBIQUITOUS CHIP** and **THAI FOUNTAIN**. Reports: 47/50/54/BEST RESTAUS).

BABY GRAND and **THE TRON CAFÉ-BAR**. Reports: 63/70/BEST BISTROS.

PATTAYA and **MATA HARI**. Reports: 108/109/FAR-EASTERN RESTAUS.

MOTHER INDIA. 221 1663. 28 Westminster Terr. Report: 93/INDIAN RESTAUS.

JUNKANOO. 248 7102. 111 Hope St. Report: 118/ROUND THE WORLD.

CAFÉ GANDOLFI. 552 6813. 64 Albion St. Report: 140/BEST TEAROOMS.

KID-FRIENDLY PLACES

133
xC5

✟ **TASHA BLANKITT:** 423 5172. 378 Cathcart Rd. Bit out of the way, but not far from Pollokshaws Rd on the S-side. A friendly spot to take the kids, commandeer a comfy corner and have some macaroni cheese. High chairs and half portions. 7 days, 8.30am-5.30pm (Sun 10.30am-4.30pm). (151/BEST TEAROOMS)

134
AROUND
GLASGOW
D2

✟ **BLACK BULL HOTEL, KILLEARN:** 01360 550215. Main sq in village on A81 towards Aberfoyle. Gr pub food (406/OUTSIDE GLASGOW), but esp if you've got kids and a fine day. Enclosed gdn and adventure playground in parkland out the back. Ancient oaks, a Tarzan slide and views of distant hills. Sound nice? You'd better believe it. You'll all be happy here. 7 days.

135
D3

TGI FRIDAYS: 221 6996. 113 Buchanan St. The Glas branch of the national chain adored by kids because of the way they get fussed over and are given, pretty much, a free run of the place. The food is from everywhere via America and when added, free-hand, to the crayon drawings on the tablecoth, can look quite spectacular. Huge range of cocktails available for parents who may need them. 7 days, 11am-11.30pm, Sun until 11pm.

136
C4

HARRY RAMSDEN'S: Paisley Rd W, beside motorway flyover – not far from centre, but difficult without a car. Not a bad branch of the national chain that caters well for kids. Greasy, cooked in lard and in cheerfully tacky surroundings, the chips and peas, sausage and fishcakes come in kids' portions and there's a playground to throw them into before you get back in the car.

137
A1, xC5
D4

DI MAGGIO'S: 334 8560. 61 Ruthven Lane, off Byres Rd, W End; 632 4194, 1038 Pollokshaws Rd, on a busy corner S of the river; and 248 2111, 21 Royal Exchange Sq. Bustling, friendly pizza joints with good Italian attitude to bairns. There's a choice to defy the most finicky kid. High chairs, special menu. 7 days.

138
A1

JACK McPHEES: 285 Byres Rd. Squeaky booths, gingham table covers . . . Cuthbert, Dibble and grub. Kids' meal and drink £1.95. beat that you MacBurger Wimpy King Huts! 6 days, 8am-10pm, Sun until 7pm. (161/CAFÉS)

THE BEST TEAROOMS AND COFFEE SHOPS

✝ ✝ **FRATELLI SARTI:** 248 2228. 133 Wellington St and 121 Bath St. Full report: 72/ITALIAN RESTAUS, but mentioned here just in case you want a light snack or an excellent cappuccino – and you miss it. 8am-10pm. Cl Sun.

139
D3

✝ **CAFÉ GANDOLFI:** 552 6813. 64 Albion St, Merchant City nr City Halls. The vaguely bohemian, Europe-somewhere atmos, the stained glass and the heavy, over-sized wooden furniture create a unique ambience that has stood the fashionability test of recent times. The food is light and imaginative and served all day. You may have to queue (because it's good). 7 days, 9am-11.30pm, Sun from 12noon. (178/SUNDAY BREAKFAST)

140
E4

✝ **THE GRANARY:** 226 3770. 82 Howard St, beside/behind the glass-pyramid of the St Enoch Centre towards river. A calm oasis away from the bustling shoppers on Argyle St that serves mainly vegn dishes but the emphasis is on home-baking. The apple pie is still the best in town. Hard to believe that this place exists in an area decimated by the mall-mongers. *Vive la resistance!* Mon-Sat 8.30am-6pm, Sun 11-5pm.

141
D4

✝ **CAFÉ ALBA:** 61 Otago St. Just after the dog-leg on this busy st that's always in danger of falling into the river you'll find this supremely unruffled little café. Fresh vegn fare, none of which exists much beyond lunchtime, and home-baked cakes that also have a tendency to disappear quickly. Draws a slightly arty (but not starving in garrets obviously) crowd. Mon-Sat 10am-5pm. (132/VEGN RESTAUS)

142
B1

✝ **JAVA CAFÉ:** 337 6814. 152 Park Rd, corner of Gibson St in bohemian W End. Neighbourhood caff with art and Internet (6 terminals) and famous all-day breakfast. Snacks and daily specials on-line. 7 days. 9am-10pm.

143
B2

THE METRO: Cresswell Lane, off Byres Rd nr Hillhead Stn. The huge sky-lights make this split-level rm a cheery rendezvous even on a dull day. There's a salad bar and a board for the day's hot dishes, lots of imported tortes and tarts and a weird counter system that we've never figured out. Mon-Sat 8am-6pm.

144
A1

145
C3, D4

THE WILLOW TEAROOMS: 217 Sauchiehall St. Another level (The Gallery), has been added upstairs, and a new sister tearoom has now opened at 97 Buchanan St. Both, under the discerning eye of proprietor Anne Mulhern, recreate the interiors of the original Miss Cranston's Tearooms, designed by C.R. Mackintosh. 30 blends of loose-leaf tea, all manner of cakes, scones and sandwiches and now, hold on . . . a wee glass of wine. Mon-Sat 9.30am-4.30pm. (318/MACKINTOSH)

146
D3

CAFÉ ROBERTA: 204 0860. 84 Gordon St, opp main canopied entrance to Central Stn. Popular downtown foodstop and famous cappuccino on your way to the train (or the work). 7 days. Mon-Sat 7.30am-10.30pm, Sun 10.30am-7pm. (163/COFFEE)

147
xA5

EXHIBITION CAFÉ: 353 4799. 10 Dumbreck Rd, Bellahouston Park. On the ground floor of House for an Art Lover (320/MACKINTOSH). This bright rm has a modern Spanish feel; tan leather couches, tubular steel chairs and gallery space. Nicely prepared, light, lunch menu without too much fussiness, like the surroundings. Excellent latte/espresso/cappuccino. Daily 10am-5pm.

148
C3

BRADFORDS: 245 Sauchiehall St. Coffee shop/restau upstairs from the flagship shop of this local and estimable bakery chain. Not the speediest waitresses but the macaroni cheese is close to mum's and the cakes and pies from downstairs represent Scottish bakery at its best. Mon-Sat 9am-5.30pm.

149
D3

PICKERING AND INGLIS, THE CHAPTERHOUSE: 26 Bothwell St. A self-serve coffee shop at the back of a bookshop. Wholesome and home-baked; busy Christian rendezvous, behind the tracts and concordances. Mon-Sat 8.30am-4.30pm.

150
D3

THE JENNY TRADITIONAL TEAROOMS: 20 Royal Exchange Sq and opp new Gallery of Modern Art. Trad they are; inside, a chintzy parlour just as you might like to imagine it (though not perhaps off a main st in Glas). Sombrely lit and low-voiced for the serious business of taking tea (several varieties) with scones, cakes (not all home-made – tut-tut) and their famous fudge. Hot dishes and interesting sandwiches. Pavement tables in summer. Also suppers, Thu-Sat.

TASHA BLANKITT: 423 5172. 378 Cathcart Rd. An out-of-the-way and unusual gift/coffee shop/bistro S of the river with a loyal following. 'Hampstead in Govanhill' home cooking that's truthful, often imaginative and selective; micro's only there to heat things up. Mon-Sat 8.30am-5.30pm, Sun 10.30am-4.30pm. Dinner w/ends only, 7-11pm. (133/KID-FRIENDLY)

151
xC5

CCA: 350 Sauchiehall St. Within the Centre for Contemporary Arts, where there's a bookshop, exhib space and usually gr stuff going on. Bar and bistro/coffee shop; interesting and interested (possibly even in you) folk. 9am-11pm/12midnight. Cl Sun. (325/NIGHTLIFE)

152
C3

LA FOCACCIA: 337 1642. 291 Byres Rd. Italian coffee shop on busy Byres Rd with freshly-made sandwiches on a variety of continental breads, strong java and appetising cakes and pastries. Those tiny wrought-iron and polished wood island thingies to perch at and babelicious counter staff – all gals . . . this is, after all, an Italian gaff. Soaves ice cream. Mon-Sat 7am-11pm, Sun 9am-10pm.

153
A1

COSTA COFFEE: 221 9305. Royal Exchange Sq. For some reason they haven't given themselves a door number, so if you're facing the statue of the Duke of Wellington, resplendent in his crowning glory (a traffic cone!), it's on your right. The expanded version of the regular coffee house. All the steamy noises and aromas, double filled sarnies, etc. plus flapjacks and some hot dishes, but coffee is the business; a swift espresso should see you round the Gallery of Modern Art (264/OTHER ATTRACTIONS) in no time.

154
D3

GREAT CAFÉS AND GREASY SPOONS

155
A2

✝ ✝ **UNIVERSITY CAFÉ:** 87 Byres Rd. When your granny, in the lines of the well-known song, was 'shoved aff a bus', this is where she was taken afterwards and given a wee cup of tea to steady her nerves. People have been coming here for generations to sit at the 'kneesy' tables and share the salt and vinegar. Run by the Verecchia family who administer advice, sympathy and pie, beans and chips with equal aplomb. A gem. Daily until 10pm (w/ends until 10.30pm). Cl Tue. Takeaway open later.

156
xC5

✝ ✝ **THE UNIQUE:** 223 Allison St. Not exactly central, but if you're on the S-side you'll find the best fish 'n' chips in town here. Through the curtain in the café they serve lunches, fish teas and spam fritters. Veg oil used. Old-fashioned hrs, viz 8.15am-1.15pm, 3.45-9pm. That's right, 9pm – closed.

157
A1

✝ **GROSVENOR CAFÉ:** 35 Ashton Lane, behind Byres Rd nr Hillhead Stn. For over 30yrs they've been serving hot, filled rolls and bowls of steaming broth to students, and all the rest of us who have happily crammed into the wee booths. New patio at rear and licence. More extensive suppery menu after 7pm. 7 days, 9am-11pm (Mon until 7pm, Sun until 5.30pm).

158
C3

✝ **EQUI:** 449 Sauchiehall St. This used to be a schoolboy hideout when the old High School was round the corner in Elmbank St. Dogging double maths for a bacon roll and a frothy coffee in the booth at the back seemed like a fair exchange at the time. Real Formica. Few tables, erratic service; quite indispensable. Mon-Sat 10am-8pm. Cl Sun.

159
xE4

✝ **COIA'S CAFÉ:** 473 Duke St. Since 1928, supplying this E End high st with ice cream, gr deal breakfasts and the kind of comforting lunch (you would call it dinner) café-bar places just cannot do. There's a telly in the corner but it's really only there to spark off open debate. Sit-in or takeaway. Sweeties of all sorts; and Havana cigars. 7 days, 7.30am-9pm (LO 7.30pm); Sun from 11am.

160
xA5

ALLAN'S SNACK BAR: 6 Storie St, Paisley. Off the High St, a chip shop with classic greasy spoon adj and a chips-with-everything menu in a Paisley days-gone-by atmos. Happy waitresses. Mon-Thu 11am-7pm, Fri-Sat 11am-8pm. Cl Sun.

161

JACK McPHEES: 285 Byres Rd. Report: 138/KID-FRIENDLY.

THE BEST CUPS OF COFFEE

FRATELLI SARTI: 248 2228. 133 Wellington St and adj round the corner in Bath St. More a foodstop and all-round Italian experience than merely a good cup of coffee, but for many the essential hit of the day. 8am-10pm. Cl Sun (72/ITALIAN RESTAUS).

162
D3

CAFÉ ROBERTA: 204 0860. 84 Gordon St, by Central Stn. Homemade food and coffee to go (or eat in). TV foodshow recently voted it the best cup of cappuccino in the N. *La cimbali* (their coffee machine) does the business; somebody sprinkles the chocolate. Mon-Sat 7.30am-10.30pm, Sun 10.30am-7pm. (146/BEST TEAROOMS)

163
D3

LITTLE ITALY: 339 6287. 205 Byres Rd. *The King of Coffees.* Ignore the takeaway version, stand at the window, lean on the marble bar and enjoy a gulp of the Byres Rd. Mon-Thu 8am-10pm, Fri/Sat 8am-1am, Sun 5-10pm. (86/PIZZA, 189/TAKEAWAY)

164
A1

EXHIBITION CAFÉ: 353 4799. 10 Dumbreck Rd, Bellahouston Park. Café/gallery in the House for an Art Lover (320/MACKINTOSH). Quality latte/espresso/cappuccino. Daily 10am-5pm. (147/BEST TEAROOMS)

165
xA5

COSTA COFFEE AT WATERSTONE'S: 332 9105. Sauchiehall St precinct. The new coffee shop in a bookshop experience – this one an oasis in the basement of the flagship emporium. Costas everywhere but always a reliably good caffeine experience. Here you sip as you sink into a couch and flick through a book you don't have to buy – like this one! 8am-10pm, Sat until 8pm, Sun 10.30am-7pm.

166
D3

CAFFE LATTE: 553 2553. 58 Virginia St. Busy, bright and colourful (may include the clientele) corner of the gay quarter. High, comfy banquettes/narrow 'shelf' tables (more intimate rm to the rear). 'Design your own' pizza/salad, variety of breads and fillings; jugs of cocktails and big cups of creamy latte. 7 days, 8am-12midnight, Sat-Sun from 11am. (353/GAY GLAS)

167
D4

MASSIMO: 332 3227. 57 Elmbank St. Downstairs and across the street from King's Theatre, this family-run café/bar/ristorante has good pizza (88/PIZZA), an open, typically Italian attitude and strong infusions. Mon-Sat 9.30am-11.30pm. Cl Sun.

168
C3

SEATTLE COFFEE CO: 248 5757. 13 Renfield St. Riding the coffee revival. The national chain in the downtown spot. Sit in or 'to go'. 12 flavours of latte, and all the old, and new, favourites. Mon-Fri 7am-7pm, Sat 8am-6pm, Sun 10am-6pm.

169
D3

THE BEST LATE-NIGHT RESTAURANTS

170
B2

✝ **INSOMNIA/CRISPINS DELI:** 564 1700. 38 Woodlands Rd. 24hr café/deli that dispenses food, infusions, strong coffee and drinks to those who just *will not go to their beds*. In a rm full of higgledy-piggledy bits of furniture, baths full of goldfish and a clock noticeable by its absence, Glasgow's demi-monde plot and sip tea into the wee hrs of the afternoon. 7 days, 24hr.

171
C4

CHANGE AT JAMAICA: 429 4422. 11-17 Clyde Pl, under railway br. A café/restau which comes into its own after midnight on Fri/Sat. 'Breakfast' (anything from porridge to pizza) until 5am for night owls and party animals – an essential slice of Glas nightlife. You may have to wait for a table once the club crowd arrive (from 3am on). Drinks until 1am. Also lunch and 7pm-12midnight. Cl Sun.

172
C3

CANTON EXPRESS: 332 0145. 407 Sauchiehall St. A bit forlorn these days since their chef left for pastures new, but still open late and still serving hot, tasty food to those that know what they want and want it now. 7 days 12noon-4am.

173
C3

THE NOODLE BAR: 333 1883. 482 Sauchiehall St. And this is where the chef went (across the rd next door to the The Garage). The real deal. Authentic, Chinese fast food, no frills (ticket service and eezee-kleen tables). The noodle is 'king' here; cooking is taken seriously. 7 days, 12noon-5am. (106/FAR-EASTERN RESTAUS)

174
C3

KING'S CAFÉ: 332 0898. 71 Elmbank St. Here for yrs, for that special, deep-fried pizza need that sometimes, inexplicably, gets you at 3am. Restau until 11pm; takeaway until 4.30am Thu/Fri/Sat.

175
E4

GUIDO'S CORONATION RESTAURANT: 552 3994. 55 Gallowgate. Nr the Barrowland for as long as people have been going there. Fish and chips and home-made pizza/ice cream. Sit-in or takeaway. Sun-Thu until 1am, Fri-Sat until 2am.

176
C4

PRINCE ARMANY'S: 420 6660. 7 Clyde Pl. Over Jamaica St Br and under the railway br on the rt, adj Change at Jamaica (*see above*). Glasgow's Arabic restau that transforms into a club with guest DJs after 12midnight. Tue-Fri 5pm-12midnight, w/ends until 5am. Cl Mon. (119/ROUND THE WORLD)

177
D3

FROGGIE'S: 332 8790. 53 W Regent St. Order by 11pm, but this French/cajun caff/bistro is open 7 days until 1am. (122/FRENCH)

GOOD PLACES FOR SUNDAY BREAKFAST

✚ CAFÉ GANDOLFI: 552 6813. 64 Albion St. Atmospheric rm, with soft daylight filtering through the stained glass and the comforting, oversized wooden furniture. This is a pleasant start to another Sunday, that day of rest made even better with some baked eggs, a pot of tea and the Sun papers. From 11am. (140/BEST TEA-ROOMS)

178
E4

BAY TREE: 403 Gr Western Rd. This excellent caff (128/VEGN RESTAUS) provides another antidote to the toxins of Sat night. A hearty vegan breakfast is served all day. From 11am.

179
B1

COTTIER'S: 93 Hyndland St, off Hyndland Rd. Off the top of Hyndland St nr Highburgh Rd. Deep in the hefty-mortgage belt of Hyndland, this converted church probably gets more of a congregation now than it ever did. Eclectic menu from fruit plate to the full monty and eggs benedict to cajun kedgeree. 12noon-4pm. Papers provided. (64/BEST BISTROS)

180
A1

CUL DE SAC: 44 Ashton Lane, off Byres Rd. A smart relaxed place to phase into Sun. Clubby staff, so revival may take until late afternoon. The fry-up includes potato scones and comes in a vegn version, and there are the better-than-average burgers and exotic crêpes. Brunch 12noon-4pm. (67/BEST BISTROS)

181
A1

NICO'S: 332 5736. 379 Sauchiehall St. Long-established example of the French café-bar abroad. Begins to look like a Manet painting in late-afternoon light ('Oh, c'mon Graeme!'). Croissants, cafetieres and comfy banquettes. Brunch: 12noon-4pm (open until 12midnight).

182
C3

UPSTAIRS AT THE CHIP: 334 5007. 12 Ashton Lane. 'Sair heid' or not, their Bloody Marys are the best in town and combined with a veggie breakfast (gr potato crowdie), famously restorative. Selection of papers. Unhurried. From 12.30pm. (69/BEST BISTROS)

183
A1

SAL E PEPE: 341 0999. 18 Gibson St. Report: 76/ITALIAN RESTAUS.

THE BEST TAKEAWAY PLACES

184
xC5

✝ **MISE EN PLACE:** 424 4600. 122 Nithsdale Rd. S-side specialist caterer and deli run by Suzanne Ritchie, who knows that sun-dried tomatoes are not enough. Everything from dinner *à deux* to full-on alfresco bash with cool waiters and other trimmings. Delivered to your door or drop in for delish lunch. Mon-Fri 9.15am-5.45pm, Sat 9.15am-2pm.

185
D3

✝ **HUNGRYS:** 353 1889. 98 Bath St. 'American-style' deli/sand-wich shop in downtown Glas. It's a long way from 34th St, NYC, but it's much better than most on these blocks, as long lunch queues attest. Several kinds of bread, good soup. Try a pep-per and tuna mayo on herb focaccia. Mon-Fri 8am-4pm.

186
D3

FIRST CHOICE: 331 2272. 138 Renfield St. At the top of the town, across the st from Scottish Television. Good selection of cheeses and sandwich meats – their pastrami and Swiss toastie is v popular and v Glas. Freshly-made coffee and a selection of cakes – but the empire biscuits don't last much beyond 11am. What is it about STV and empires? Mon-Fri 6.30am-5pm, Sat 6.30am-3pm.

187
D3, C3

NUMBER ONE SANDWICH ST: 248 2050, 104 St Vincent St and 221 2002, 9 Waterloo St. 2 other downtown locations where office-workers and shop assistants descend in droves for assembly-line and some bespoke sandwiches and baked potatoes. Betw them they produce over 1,000 lunches a day. Mon-Fri 8am-4pm.

188
B3

SANSIRO: 248 9553. 539 Sauchiehall St. Smart, little Italian lunch-box W of Charing Cross. Pizza, pasta, over-stuffed ciabatta, crostino and good coffee to take away in this constantly changing part of Sauchiehall St. Mon-Fri 8am-4pm.

189
A1

LITTLE ITALY: 339 6287. 205 Byres Rd. Gr pizza and pasta (86/PIZZA), freshly-baked breads, ice cream, loadsa Italian wines and a no-bad (meaning 'not at all bad') cup of coffee (164/COFFEE). Mon-Thu 8am-10pm, Fri-Sat 8am-1am, Sun 5-10pm.

190
A1

LE PETIT PAIN: 337 1118. 239 Byres Rd. Bright, little continental baguette/ciabatta shop, baking on premises. Most fillings a combi-nation of 2 or 3 ingredients and the whole effect is . . . fresh. Good coffee. Mon-Fri 8.30am-6pm, Sat 9am-6pm, Sun 12am-6pm.

191
xB1

TOSCANA: 956 4020. 46 Station Rd, Milngavie. It's a long way from town, but this family-run Italian Café does gr takeaway pasta and pizza and home-made puds. Until 10pm.

UNIVERSITY CAFÉ 'people have been coming here
for generations to sit at the "kneesy" tables'
(page 54)

FRATELLI SARTI 'Glasgow's famed *emporio d'Italia*' (page 37)

WHERE TO DRINK

SOME GREAT 'GLASGOW' PUBS

Pubs that are notable for other specific reasons are on other pages. Pubs in Glas are licensed until 12midnight or 1am (and later only during special events).

192
D4

✠ **VICTORIA BAR:** 157 Bridgegate. 'The Vicky' is in the 'Briggait', one of Glasgow's oldest streets, nr the Victoria Br over the Clyde. Once a pub for the fishmarket and open odd hrs, now it's a howff for all those who like an atmos that's old, friendly and uncontrived. Small interior; you can close the door on all that new Glas. Maclays, Theakstons and Greenmantle ales. Mon-Sat until 12midnight, Sun until 11pm. (340/FOLK MUSIC)

193
D4

✠ **SCOTIA BAR:** 112 Stockwell St. Nr the Victoria (*see above*), late-1920s Tudor-style pub with a low-beamed ceiling and intimate, woody 'snug'. Long the haunt of folk musicians, writers and raconteurs. Music and poetry sessions, folk and blues. Daily until 12midnight. (339/FOLK MUSIC)

194
D4

✠ **CLUTHA VAULTS:** 167 Stockwell St. This and the pubs above are part of the same family of trad Glas pubs. The Clutha (ancient name for the Clyde) has a Victorian-style interior and an even longer history. Music. Mon-Sat until 12midnight, Sun until 11pm. (337/FOLK MUSIC)

195
E4

✠ **BLACKFRIARS:** 36 Bell St. Contemporary version of the 'old' city's public houses, essential as meeting places, because poky tenement flats were not built for entertaining. Nowadays, there's more space, but the people are just as sociable and there's no back green. Ales, lagers old and new, all-day menu including 'nightbites' until 12midnight (231/PUB FOOD). Regular programme of music (251/LIVE MUSIC). 7 days until 12midnight.

196
D3

✠ **THE HORSESHOE:** 17 Drury St. A mighty pub since 1884 (and before) in the small st betw Mitchell and Renfrew Sts nr the stn. Early example of this style of pub, dubbed 'gin palaces'. Island rather than horseshoe bar and an upstairs lounge where they serve high-tea. The food is amazing value (225/PUB FOOD). Caledonian and Maclays. Daily until 12midnight.

197
B2

✠ **THE HALT BAR:** 160 Woodlands Rd. On the old tram route W, this Edwardian pub remains largely unspoiled. Original counter and snug intact. Home to the Bud Neill Appreciation

Society. Neill's surreal, 1950s cartoon characters have been immortalised, across the rd, in bronze. 'Mighty fine'. (202/'UNSPOILT' PUBS, 253/LIVE MUSIC) Open until 11pm (12midnight w/ends). The Halt is handily close to:

✚ **UISGE BEATHA**: 246 Woodlands Rd. 'Oo-i-skay Bay' (or something like that) means 'the water of life' and is a unique Highland outpost in the city. Shooting-lodge chic and cosy; more than a mere draught of the Gael. Good grub at lunch time. Related to one of the gr Highland bars, The Drover's Inn, Inverarnan. Sun-Thu until 11pm, Fri-Sat until 12midnight.

198
B2

BAR 10: 10 Mitchell Lane, off Buchanan St. Mongrel furniture and sliced-brawn tiles, high ceiling and design by Ben Kelly of Manchester's Hacienda fame, this place looks like it's been transported from Canal St, NYC. Good food, gossip and strong coffee served with a shot of iced water during the day; the place to go pre-club at night. Regular DJs at w/ends. (234/THESE ARE HIP)

199
D3

THE LOUNGE, THE LIVING-ROOM, THE APARTMENT: W Regent St and Byres Rd. 2 bars and a club related, not necessarily in style, but by protagonist Colin Barr's entrepreneurial vision. The Lounge in W Regent St is a beach-bar basement with football TV and a big Sun breakfast. The Living Room at the bottom of Byres Rd is a 2 rm see-and-be-seen scenario with eclectic menu (until 8pm) and smooth music. The Apartment is a relaxed, stylish, after-hrs drinking club in Royal Exchange Sq (11pm-3am Thu-Mon). Bars: 7 days until 12midnight.

200
C3, B2,
D4

McPHABBS: 23 Sandyford Pl. 2 blocks W of Charing Cross. Non-aligned boozer, more of a 'shebeen' than anything else. *Laissez-faire* attitude. Postage-stamp patio at rear, tasty bar food, endorsed by local MP George Galloway (225/PUB FOOD). Good malts. 7 days, until 12midnight Fri-Sat.

201
B3

WEST END

GREAT WESTERN ROAD

SAUCHIEHALL STREET

BYRES ROAD

DUMBARTON RD

Kelvingrove Park

Charing Cross

WOODLANDS ROAD

● 198
● 197

● 201

● 200

SECC

Bells Bridge

CLYDEBANK EXPRESSWAY

River Clyde

Kingston Bridge

BROOMIELAW

● 200

CENTRAL STATION

ST ENOCH SHOPPING CENTRE

● 196
● 200
● 199

P

QUEEN STREET STATION

BUCHANAN BUS STATION

GALLOWGATE

Glasgow Green

HIGH STREET

● 195
● 192
● 194
● 193

THE BARRAS

SALTMARKET

Victoria Bridge

Albert Bridge

River Clyde

SOUTH SIDE

BALLATER STREET

GORBALS STREET

POLLINGSHIELDS

THE BEST OLD 'UNSPOILT' PUBS

Of course it's not necessarily the case that when a pub's done up it's spoiled, or that all old pubs are worth preserving but some have resisted change and that's part of their appeal. The following places don't have to recreate 'atmos'. Most of these pubs close no later than 12midnight.

HALT BAR: 160 Woodlands Rd. Edwardian pub, that used to be an official stop on the old tram route W. In the classic trad of the stand-up bar with a 'snug' (for the ladies), behind a wooden partition, with 'pulpit' serving-hatch. Varied (free) live music through the back (253/LIVE MUSIC). Sun-Thu until 11pm, Fri-Sat until 12midnight. Music usually from 9pm. (197/GREAT GLAS PUBS)

202
B2

THE GRIFFIN (AND THE GRIFFINY AND THE GRIFFINETTE): 266 Bath St. Corner of Elmbank St nr King's Theatre. Built 1903 to anticipate the completion of the theatre and offer the patrons a pre-show pie and a pint. Stand at the Edwardian Bar like generations of Glaswegians. Main bar still retains 'snug' with a posh, etched-glass partition; booths have been added but the atmos is still 'Old Glasgow' (223/PUB FOOD). Sun-Thu until 11pm, Fri-Sat until 12midnight.

203
C3

THE ROWAN TREE, UDDINGSTON: 12km SE of centre via M74. In Old Mill Rd off Main St where sign points (in opp direction) for Bothwell Castle (380/OUTSIDE GLASGOW). A cottagey pub in the shadow of the world-famous Tunnock's Caramel Wafers factory and long frequented by the wafermakers. Food at lunchtime, coal fire in winter, folk music on Fris. Maclays. Mon-Sat until 11.45pm, Sun until 11pm.

204
xE2

THE SARACEN'S HEAD: Gallowgate, nr Barrowlands. An establishment of this name has existed in the neighbourhood since 1755, playing host to a multitude of colourful characters; not least Boswell and Johnson, on the return leg of their grand Highland tour. This, the most recent incarnation, opened in 1905 and is famous for its lethal 'White Tornado' cider. The atmos is more 'wild west' than E End, although the 'one singer, one song' rule still prevails. 7 days, but not open late (Fri-Sat until 9pm).

205
E4

THE MITRE: The lane of Brunswick St, off Argyle St opp C&A. Untouched by the 'gentryfiers' and full of character. Gem of a bar, just quietly getting on with its business. Bit of music at w/ends,

206
D4

food at lunch, Belhaven; nothing fancy. 7 days until 11pm or 12midnight.

207
xC5

M J HERAGHTY: 708 Pollokshaws Rd. More than a touch of the Irish about this pub and easily more authentic than recent imports. A local with loyal regulars who'll make you welcome; old pub practices still hold in this howff in the S. Sun-Thu until 11pm, Fri-Sat until 12midnight.

208
A5

BRECHIN'S: 803 Govan Rd. Nr jnct with Paisley Rd W and motorway over-pass. Established in 1798 and, as they say, always in the same family. A former shipyard pub which, despite the proximity to Rangers FC, is not partisan. It's behind the statue of shipbuilder Sir William Pearce (which, covered in sooty grime, was known as the 'Black Man') and there's a feline 'rat-catcher' on the roof (making it a listed building). Unaffected neighbourhood atmos. Mon-Sat until 11pm, Sun until 6.30pm.

209
B4

THE OLD TOLL BAR: 1 Paisley Rd W. Opp the site of the original Parkhouse Toll, where monies were collected for use of the 'turnpikes' betw Glas and Greenock. Opened in 1874, the original interior is still intact; the *fin de siècle* painted glass and magnificent old gantry preserved under order. A 'palace pub' classic. Real ale and some single malts. 7 days until 11pm.

210
D3

THE HORSESHOE: 17 Drury St. The celebrated city-centre bar with the famous longest bar in the world and an assortment of Old and New Glaswegians all along it. (196/GREAT GLAS PUBS, 224/PUB FOOD)

211
E4, xA5

BAIRDS BAR and THE DISTRICT: 2 bars from opp sides of the gr divide. **BAIRDS** in the Gallowgate adj Barrowlands is a Catholic stronghold green to the gills where, on days when Celtic play at home up the rd at Parkhead, you'd have to be in by 11am to get a drink. **THE DISTRICT,** 252 Paisley Rd W, Govan, nr Ibrox Park, is where Rangers supporters gather and rule in their own blue heaven. Both pubs give an extraordinary insight into what makes the Glas time bomb tick. Provided you aren't wearing the wrong colours (or say something daft), you'll be very welcome in either.

THE BEST REAL-ALE PUBS

Pubs on other pages may purvey real ale, but the following are the ones where they take it seriously and/or have a good choice.

⚓ BON ACCORD: 153 N St. On a slip rd of the motorway swathe nr the Mitchell Library. One of the first real-ale pubs in Glas. Over 100 malts as well as up to 18 beers; always Youngers 3, McEwan's 80/-, Theakston and Old Peculier, plus many guest ales on hand pump. Food at lunchtime and light bites until 9pm. Light, easy-going atmos here, but they do take their ale seriously; there's even a 'tour' of the cellars if you want it. Mon-Sat until 12midnight, Sun until 11.30pm.

212
B3

⚓ THREE JUDGES: 141 Dumbarton Rd, opp the bottom of Byres Rd. Named after the triumvirate of boxing judges that used to own it. These days you're more likely to find professors than practitioners of the 'gentlemanly art'. Maclays and 9 guest ales that change regularly (1,320 at last count). 7 days.

213
A2

TENNENTS: 191 Byres Rd. Nr the always-red traffic lights at Univ Ave, a big, booming watering-hole of a place where you're never far away from the horseshoe bar and its several excellent hand-pumped ales, incl Maclays, Caledon-ian and Theakston. Revamped to take it into the next century, but the 'old century' crowd will still be there.

214
A1

BABBITY BOWSTER: 16 Blackfriars St. In a pedestrianised part of the Merchant City and just off the High St, a highly successful pub/restau/hotel (17/INEXPENSIVE HOTELS); but the pub comes first. Maclays is heavily featured and make their own Babbity Thistle Ale, but there's always an English guest and lots of malts. Food all day (230/PUB FOOD), occasional folk music (esp Sun), o/side patio (247/DRINK OUTDOORS) and exhibs. Proprietor Fraser Laurie has thought of everything.

215
E4

BOSWELL HOTEL: 27 Mansionhouse Rd. S-side via Pollokshaws Rd, Langside Ave and rt just before the Battlefield Monument at the edge of Queen's Park. Though now passed from private hands to Tennents, purveyors of fizzy lagers, this remains a real-ale haven. 3 busy bars and notable for family pub food. Usually 3 or 4 regulars and 8 guest ales, all well looked after. Rms upstairs (good INX accom). Fine, unpretentious grub till 10pm. Kids and all non-believers welcome. Sun-Thu until 11pm, Fri-Sat until 12midnight.

216
xC5

217
D3

THE CASK AND STILL: 154 Hope St. Formerly the Pot Still, there are up to 8 ales here (always Youngers 3, McEwan's 80/- and Old Peculier), but it's also noted for a mind-boggling range of malts. They've got over 200. Mon-Sat until 11pm/12midnight. Cl Sun. Same folk have the **RITZ BAR** at 241 N St nr the Bon Accord (*see above*). Large, friendly boozer with half a dozen ales and food to go with. Occasional music and quiz nights. 7 days but cl Sun lunch.

218
A2

THE TAP: 1055 Sauchiehall St, nr Kelvingrove Park. (Formerly The Brewery Tap.) Now calling itself a Bar and Coffee Huis (just like those wee places in Amsterdam where you choose your fave mind-altering smokable from the colourfully chalked-up menu on the blackboard . . . not!). All the old posters advertising obscure jazz legends and their even more esoteric gigs have disappeared, to be replaced with . . . pine, and lots of it. Same old crowd and friendly staff though. *Plus ça change.* Belhaven, Caledonian, Arrols, Tetleys and guests.

219
xC5

THE STOAT AND FERRET: 1534 Pollokshaws Rd. S-side sister to The Tap/Blackfriars and ploughing a similar furrow. Regularly changed guest ales; featured beer of the month and live folk/jazz at the w/ends.

220
xC5

THE ATHENA TAVERNA: 778 Pollokshaws Rd. Intimate wine bar/lounge adj decent Greek restau on the S-side (114/ROUND THE WORLD) with 2 Czech beers on draft and a large selection of German wheat-beers. Restau hrs.

221
D3

THE HORSESHOE: 17 Drury St. Gr for lots of reasons (196/GREAT GLAS PUBS), not the least of which is its range of beers: Caledonian, Greenmantle, Maclays and Bass on hand pump.

222
D4

VICTORIA BAR: 157 Bridgegate. Another pub mentioned before (192/GREAT GLAS PUBS) where FPA, Maclays and others can be drunk in a dark woody atmos enlivened by occasional trad music (340/FOLK MUSIC).

PUBS WITH GOOD FOOD

Most of these pubs are also notable for other reasons. Glas bars usually close no later than 12midnight.

✚ THE GRIFFIN: 266 Bath St. On corner of Elmbank St across from King's Theatre. The Griffin, the Griffiny and the Griffinette: they're always there on that corner and your basic pie/chips/beans and a pint will not be bettered at this price (£2.50 at time of going to press, the equivalent 80yrs ago of 8 old pence). Other staples available and a more elaborate menu in the lounge or the Griffinette next door (incl Sun lunch). Food: 12noon-3pm and evenings untill 7pm. Pub until 12midnight/1am. (203/'UNSPOILT' PUBS)

223
C3

✚ THE HORSESHOE: 17 Drury St. The classic pub to be recommended for all kinds of reasons. But lunch is a particularly good deal with 3 courses for £2.40 (pie and beans 80p), and old favourites on the menu like mushy peas, macaroni cheese, jelly and fruit. Lunch 12noon-2.30pm and all afternoon upstairs, inclg high-tea until 7.30pm (not quite the same atmos, but pure Glas). Pub open daily until 12midnight. (196/GREAT GLAS PUBS)

224
D3

✚ McPHABBS: 221 0770. 23 Sandyford Pl. 2 blocks W of Charing Cross. Gr Scottish/Irish bar food; smoked haddies, salmon and steaks, beef and Guinness stew, etc. Given the 'parliamentary seal of approval' by local MP George Galloway who particularly rates the stew. 7 days, open until 12midnight at the w/ends. (201/GREAT GLAS PUBS)

225
B3

✚ OBLOMOV: 339 9177. 372 Gr Western Rd, Kelvinbridge. The latest Ron McCulloch (designer and entrepreneur of this parish). This time the timeless appeal of sepia, softly-lit prewar kinda thing. Anyone been to Prague recently? Booths and chaises, big drapes. Crepuscular dining-rm. Contemporary menu. Their food is good. 7 days. Served 11.30am-8.30pm.

226
B1

THE BIG BLUE: 445 Gr Western Rd. A modern bar/bistro in a gr uptown location literally on the (river) Kelvinside. Drinking drowns the eating later on, but until mid-evening there's excellent Italian pub grub. Big Sun breakfast.

227
B1

THE DRUM AND MONKEY: 93 St Vincent St, on corner of Renfield St. Cavernous but comfortable and particularly successful bar/bistro with a sombre gentlemen's club atmos – 'the odd libation for the overworked'. Comfort and more contemporary food with a bistro

228
D3

through the back which has an à la carte menu in the evening. Puds on blackboard. Also in Edin. 7 days until 11pm.

229
A2

MURPHY'S PAKORA: 1287 Argyle St. A good idea (long ago sold on) which solves the problem of what to drink with spicy Indian food (Murphy's Irish Stout). Pakora (best in mixed selections of 'thalis' or platters where you can choose any 3) are served all day; gram flour batter wrapped round anything you can think of (incl haggis) dipped in 3 sauces. Moist bits like aubergines and seafood work best. Table service and bar. 7 days, LO 11pm.

230
E4

BABBITY BOWSTER: 16 Blackfriars St. Already listed as a pub for real ale and as a hotel (there are rms upstairs), the food is mentioned mainly for its Scottishness (haggis and stovies) and all-day availability. It's also pleasant to eat o/side on the patio/grd in summer. Breakfast is served from 8am. (215/REAL-ALE PUBS, 17/INEXPENSIVE HOTELS)

231
E4

BLACKFRIARS: 36 Bell St. Candleriggs is one of the focal points in the Merchant City. Gr Glas pub for all-round ambience, provision of real ale and music, and food available all day until 12midnight (but drinkers loud after 9pm). Menu changes slightly for evenings, but it's mainly pub-grub favourites such as the ubiquitous potato skins and Death by Chocolate. Specials vary with staff, who's cooking, etc. (195/GREAT GLAS PUBS, 251/LIVE MUSIC)

232
D4

RAB HA'S: 572 0400. 83 Hutcheson St. In an area bristling with pubs and eateries this old Merchant City howff has a reputation for good food. Well-chosen selection of bar meals, incl organic veg specials. Restau downstairs in the evening. This place gets better and better. (15/INEXPENSIVE HOTELS)

233
xA5

FOX AND HOUNDS, HOUSTON: On B790 village main st in Renfrewshire, 30km W of centre by M8 jnct 29 (A726), then cross back under motorway on B790. Village pub with real fire and dining-rm upstairs for family meals and suppers. Folk come from miles around. Sun roasts. Gr example of couthie cuisine. Food available daily at lunchtime and from 6-10pm (all day Sat-Sun).

THESE ARE HIP

BAR 10: 221 8353. 10 Mitchell Lane, halfway up Buchanan St pedestrian precinct on the left. There's an NYC look about this joint that is so loved by its habitues, they make an exhib out of themselves. Designed by Ben Kelly of Hacienda fame, after 5yrs it has stood the fashion test and is as happening as ever. Good pre-club spot. Play it again Sam! (199/GREAT GLAS PUBS)

234
D4

BARGO: 553 4771. 80 Albion St. In the Merchant City, this spacious, designer-theque is much in demand for fashion shoots and, of course, high-glam posing on a Sat night. Can be attractively, if not spookily, quiet during the week when surprisingly OK food is served. (71/BEST BISTROS)

235
E4

BAR MIRO: 353 0475. 36 Kelvingrove St. Nr Kelvingrove Park, off Sauchiehall St. Stylish bar on 2 floors that spills out onto the steps and a tiny forecourt in warm weather. Decent bar food if you fancy something light before tripping the light fantastic.

236
A3

CUL DE SAC: 649 4717. 44 Ashton Lane. This upstairs bar is a perennial W End fave. Close to the underground for that last-minute dash into town to beat club curfews. (67/BEST BISTROS)

237
A1

MOJO: 331 2257. 158a Bath St. City centre, underground bar with comfy couches and a smart, urban atmos. Good food through the back (62/BEST BISTROS). DJs obliterate the food thing, but raise the temperature later on.

238
D3

MONKEY BAR: 353 2351. 100 Bath St. Colourful, underground bar, nr Mojo (*see above*). Busy at the w/ends with a young professional/student crowd.

239
D3

POLO LOUNGE: 553 1221. 84 Wilson St. Urbane and stylish bar/disco by the irrepressible Stephen King. Latest fave on the gay scene in the heart of the emerging quarter. Clubbable rather than clubby crowd until late on arranged around the comfortable furniture. Mellow Sun afternoons; papers and jazz. (347/GAY GLAS)

240
D4

YO YO: 248 8484. 31 Queen St. Sports-themed, neon-lit style bar for trendy young things. Next door to Archaos (358/BEST CLUBS) and with surprisingly good restau downstairs. May seem clinical/spartan for some tastes; it's the antithesis of the old Glas pub. This is for the generation who take Sky TV for granted.

241
D4

THE GATE: 333 0250. 408 Sauchiehall St. Intimate and smart, with a fondness for tartan and flavoured vodka.

242
C3

PLACES TO DRINK OUTDOORS

243
xB1

LOCK 27: 1100 Crow Rd. At the very N end of Crow Rd beyond Anniesland, an unusual boozer for Glas: a canal side pub on a lock of the Forth and Clyde Canal (273/WALKS IN THE CITY), a touch English (a v wee touch), where of a summer's day you can sit o/side. Excellent bar food, always busy. 7 days.

244
A1

COTTIER'S: 357 5825. 93 Hyndland St. First on the left after the swing park on Highburgh Rd (going W) and the converted church is on your rt, around the corner. Gr place for many reasons (64/BEST BISTROS, 180/SUNDAY BREAKFAST), but a cold beer on a hot day sitting in leafy shade is one of the best; or into the evening – life can be good! 7days.

245
xA2

WICKETS HOTEL: 334 9334. 52 Fortrose St. Probably best app via Dumbarton Rd, turning up Peel St before railway br. O/looking W of Scotland Cricket Ground (hence name). Large terr beer grd, made for long summer afternoons. You can at least imagine the thwack of balls in the distance. Good place to bring kids, even if you don't see them very often (Dad!). 7 days. (18/INEXPENSIVE HOTELS)

246
A1

JINTY McGINTY'S: 339 0747. Ashton Lane. As soon as the sun comes out, so do the punters. With the **CUL DE SAC** and **BAR BREL** at one end and Jinty's at the other, benches suddenly appear and the whole lane becomes a cobbled, alfresco pub. It's the nearest Glas gets to Euro, even Dublin, drinking. 7 days.

247
E4

BABBITY BOWSTER: 552 5055. 16 Blackfriars St. Unique, in the Merchant City for several reasons (215/REAL-ALE PUBS, 230/PUB FOOD), but in summer certainly for its napkin of grd in an area bereft of greenery. Though enclosed by surrounding sts, it's an oasis many head for. Feels like Soho, Soho NYC. Naw, feels like Glas. Always good crack. 7 days.

PUBS AND CLUBS WITH GOOD LIVE MUSIC

Many other places have live music but programmes and policies can vary quickly. Best to look out for posters or consult The List *magazine, on sale fortnightly in the city centre.*

✚ **KING TUT'S WAH WAH HUT:** 221 5279. 272 St Vincent St. Every bit as good as its namesake in Alphabet City used to be; real, edgy, make-or-break atmos in the cramped rm upstairs where bands on the club circuit play to a damp and appreciative crowd. See flyers for bigger bands coming through. Doors open 8.30pm. Tickets at bar or Tower Records, Argyle St.

248
C3

NICE 'N' SLEAZY: 333 9637. 421 Sauchiehall St at the W End. Not esp sleazy and fairly rock 'n' roll. Popular art school hang-out. Every flavour of alco-pop and voddie to drink. Good indie jukebox and play station for hire. Bands downstairs (esp Thu-Sun) with a nominal entrance charge. Usually from 9pm.

249
C3

THE CATHOUSE: 248 6606. 15 Union St, and **THE GARAGE**, Sauchiehall St, W End (same owners). Live rock clubs with mixed programme on various nights depending on availability of touring bands (other 'clubs' on other nights). Recent broadening of musical taste so no longer necessary to turn up with leather strides and pointy boots. Tickets in advance, as for King Tut's (*see above*).

250
D4, (

BLACKFRIARS: 552 5924. 36 Bell St. Merchant City pub with everything (195/GREAT GLAS PUBS) which includes all kinds of live music and, if you are a player, 'Glasgow songwriters' on Tue nights features an open mic guest policy. Turn up early to book your spot. Free. (231/PUB FOOD)

251
E4

SCOTIA BAR and THE CLUTHA VAULTS: 552 8681/552 7520. Nr each other in the E End nr the river and under same management (112 and 167 Stockwell St). Integral part of the Glas folk scene for yrs (337/339/FOLK MUSIC), but also readings and other sessions (e.g. Clutha has bluegrass and country). Glas Folk Club on Wed at Scotia and always at w/ends. Free. (193/194/GREAT GLAS PUBS)

252
D4

HALT BAR: 564 1527. 160 Woodlands Rd. Gr pub rock atmos with booked live acts on Thu and 'open mic' spots on Wed and Sat. Music starts around 9pm and admn is free. (197/GREAT GLAS PUBS, 202/'UNSPOILT' PUBS)

253
B2

254
A1

COTTIER'S: 357 5825. 93 Hyndland St. In the densely populated quadrant betw Dumbarton Rd and Byres Rd. A neighbourhood atmos to this converted church (not in, but off the top of Hyndland St nr Highburgh Rd); it has the same management as the Baby Grand (63/BEST BISTROS) and Cathedral House (11/INEXPENSIVE HOTELS). Restau upstairs (64/BEST BISTROS). Bar and theatre, on the ground level, serve as a platform for local talent and cult-ish acts from abroad. Regularly features special gigs with 3 or more bands on the bill and, occasionally, entire, musically-themed, w/ends. Good programming.

255
D4

THE 13th NOTE: 221 0414. Clyde St. New venture for the café/club that used to be in Glassford St, now divided in 2 with the vegn restau in King St (127/VEGN RESTAUS) and the gig thing down nr the river. Various combos of the indie or merely hip variety. This is the one to watch. Tue-Sun 8pm-3.30am.

ROGANO 'an institution in Glasgow since the 1930s' (page 29)

MUSEUM OF TRANSPORT 'one of Scotland's most fascinating museums' (page 81)

WHERE TO GO IN TOWN

KELVINGROVE ART GALLERY AND MUSEUM 'huge Victorian sand-stone edifice with awesome atrium' (page 79)

THE MAIN ATTRACTIONS

✝ ✝ **KELVINGROVE ART GALLERY AND MUSEUM:** 287 2700. At westerly extension of Argyle St and Sauchiehall St by Kelvingrove Park. Huge Victorian sandstone edifice with awesome atrium. On the ground floor is a natural history/Scottish history museum. The upper salons contain the city's superb British and European art collection. There are strong contemporary exhibs as well as the permanent collection. Pipe-organ recitals every alternate Sun. Tearoom. The Museum of Transport (262/OTHER ATTRACTIONS) is across the rd. Mon-Sat 10am-5pm, Sun from 11am. (311/BEST ARCHITECTURE) FREE

256
A2

✝ ✝ **THE BURRELL COLLECTION and POLLOK PARK:** 649 7151. S of river via A77 Kilmarnock Rd (over Jamaica St Br) about 5km, following signs from Pollokshaws Rd. Set in rural parkland, this hugely successful attraction is an award-winning modern gallery built to house the eclectic acquisitions of Sir William Burrell. Showing a preference for medieval works, among the 8,500 items the magpie magnate donated to the city in 1944 are artefacts from the Roman empire to Rodin. The building itself integrates old doorways and whole rms reconstructed from Hutton Castle. Self-serve café and restau on the ground floor. Pollok House and Grds further into the park (with works by Goya, El Greco and William Blake) is worth a detour and has, below stairs, the better tearoom. Both open Mon-Sat 10am-5pm, Sun from 11am. Cl Tue. (274/WALKS IN THE CITY) FREE

257
xC5

✝ **GLASGOW CATHEDRAL / PROVAND'S LORDSHIP:** 552 8198/552 8819. High St. Across the rd from one another they represent what remains of the oldest part of the city, which (as can be seen in the People's Palace, *see below*) was, in the early 18th century, merely a ribbon of streets from here to the river. The present Cathedral, though established by St Mungo in AD 543, dates from the 12th century and is a fine example of the v real, if gloomy, Gothic. The house, built in 1471, is a museum which strives to convey a sense of medieval life. Watch you don't get run over when you re-emerge into the 20th century and try to cross the st. In the background, the Necropolis piled on the hill invites inspection and offers a viewpoint and the full Gothic perspective. Cl Tues.

258
xE3

✝ **THE PEOPLE'S PALACE:** 554 0223. Reopened after renovations in spring 1998. App via the Tron and London Rd, then turn rt into Glas Green. This has been a folk museum *par excellence* where-

259
E5

in, since 1898, the history, folklore and artefacts of a proud city have been gathered, cherished and displayed. But this is much more than a mere museum; it is the heart and soul of the city and together with the Winter Grds adj, shouldn't be missed if you want to know what Glasgow's about. Tearoom in the Tropics, among the palms and ferns of the Winter Grds, will still be part of the attraction for any visitor in the future. Opening times will be as other museums (*see above*). FREE

260
xE3

ST MUNGO MUSEUM OF RELIGIOUS LIFE AND ART: 553 2557. In the Cathedral precinct or sq dubbed 'Ft Weetabix' by Glas cabbies. Opened with some gnashing of teeth and wringing of hands in 1993, it houses art and artefacts representing the world's 6 major religions arranged tactfully in an attractive stone building with a Zen grd in the courtyard. The dramatic Dalì *Crucifixion* seems somehow lost, and the assemblage seems like a good and worthwhile vision not quite realised. But if you like your spirituality shuffled but not stirred, this is for you. The punters' comments board is always . . . enlightening. Mon-Sat 10-5pm, Sun from 11am. Cl Tues. FREE

261
B2

HUNTERIAN MUSEUM AND GALLERY: 330 5431. Univ Ave. On one side of the st, Glasgow's oldest museum with geological, archaeological and social history displayed in a venerable building. The cloisters outside and the **UNIVERSITY CHAPEL** should not be missed. Across the st, a modern block contains part of Glasgow's exceptional civic collection – Rembrandt to the Colourists and the Glasgow Boys, as well as one of the most complete collections of any artist's work and personal effects to be found anywhere, viz that of Whistler. It's fascinating stuff, even if you're not a fan. There's also a print gallery and the superb **MACKINTOSH HOUSE** (316/MACKINTOSH). Mon-Sat 9.30am-5pm. FREE

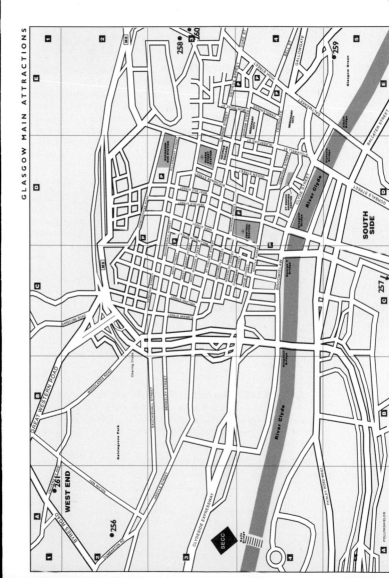

GLASGOW MAIN ATTRACTIONS

THE OTHER ATTRACTIONS

262
A2

✝ ✝ **MUSEUM OF TRANSPORT:** 287 2700. Off Argyle St behind the Kelvin Hall and opp Art Gallery. May not seem your ticket to ride, but this is one of Scotland's most fascinating museums. Has something for everybody, esp kids. The reconstruction of a cobbled Glas st *circa* 1938 is an inspired evocation. There are trains, trams and unique collections of cars, motorbikes and bicycles. And model ships in the Clyde rm, in remembrance of a mighty river. Make a donation and the Mini splits in two. Mon-Sat 10am-5pm, Sun 11am-5pm.   FREE

263
xB1

✝ ✝ **BOTANIC GARDENS AND KIBBLE PALACE:** 334 2422. Gr Western Rd. Smallish park close to R Kelvin with riverside walks (272/WALKS IN THE CITY), and pretty much the 'dear green place'. Kibble Palace (built 1873) is the distinctive domed glasshouse with statues set among lush ferns and shrubbery from around the (mostly temperate) world. A wonderful place to muse and wander. Grds open till dusk; palace 10am-4.45pm.

264
D4

✝ ✝ **GALLERY OF MODERN ART:** 331 1854. Queen St. Central, controversial and housed in former Stirling Library, Glasgow's newest big visual arts attraction opened in a hail of art world bickering in 1996. Director Julian Spalding's choice of inclusion raised to record levels both the ire of critics and the interest of the public. This 'Modern Art' incl contemporary and populist from elsewhere, but little from the influential movements and bugger all from the Saatchi side in which many Glas artists have made notable contributions. Smart café up top. Check hrs.   FREE

265
xE4

✝ ✝ **THE BARROWS:** (pronounced 'Barras') The sprawling st and indoor market area in the E End of the city around the Gallowgate. An experience, an institution, a slice of pure Glas. If you're only in town for one w/end, it's a must, and like no other market anywhere. Sat and Sun only.

266
C2

✝ ✝ **THE TENEMENT HOUSE:** 333 0183. 145 Buccleuch St. Nr Charing Cross but can app from nr the end of Sauchiehall St and over the hill. The typical 'respectable' Glas tenement kept under a bell-jar since Our Agnes moved out in 1965. She had lived there with her mother since 1911 and wasn't one for new-fangled things. It's a touch claustrophobic, with hordes of visitors, and is distinctly voyeuristic, but, well . . . your house would be interesting, too, in 50yrs time if the clock were stopped. Daily, Mar-Oct 2-5pm.   ADMN

POLLOK LEISURE CENTRE: 881 3313. Cowglen Rd. Adj Pollok shopping centre in S-side. From city centre take Pollokshaws Rd, then rt fork (after 3km) to Pollok Park and rt (after 1km) at r/bout along Barrhead Rd. Centre is 2km along on left at next r/bout. A place to take kids for water immersion thrills, slides, etc in modern, safe leisurama. Mon-Fri 9.30am-9pm, Sat-Sun 10am-4pm.

267
xC5

GREENBANK GARDENS: 10km SW of centre via Kilmarnock Rd, Eastwood Toll, Clarkston Toll and Mearns Rd. Then signposted (3km). A spacious oasis in the suburbs; formal grds and 'working' walled grd, parterre and woodland walks around elegant Georgian house. V Scottish. Grds open AYR dawn-dusk, shop/tearoom Apr-Oct 11am-5pm.   NTS

268
xC5

MITCHELL LIBRARY: 287 2999. N St. On a slip rd and o/looking the canyon of the M8, the landmark domed edifice of Glasgow's main library. Named after Stephen Mitchell, tobacco lord (1789-1874), who wanted to leave a building 'worthy of the city', it opened in 1911. Interesting just to wander through the vast halls or upstairs to the quieter reading rms; the dome itself is astonishing. Theatre next door has a mixed theatre/music programme. Café until 4.30pm. Library: Mon-Fri 9am-9pm, Sat until 5pm. Cl Sun.

269
B3

CITY CHAMBERS: 287 2000. George Sq. The hugely impressive building along the whole E end of Glasgow's municipal central sq. Let's face it, it's not often that one could seriously recommend a visit to the District Council offices, but this is a wonderfully over-the-top monument to the days when Glas was the second city of the empire, a cross between an Italian Renaissance palace and an Escher marble maze. Guided tours Mon-Fri, 10.30am and 2.30pm.

270
E3

FINLAYSTONE ESTATE: 01475 540505. 30km W of city centre via fast M8/A8, signed off dual carriageway just before Pt Glas. Delightful grds and woods around mansion house with many pottering places and longer trails (and ranger service). Various 'attractions', e.g. that rare thing: a walled grd and Victorian laundry and kitchen, etc. Visitor centre and conservatory tearoom. Much better family outing than McDonalds or the grd centre. 7 days, 10.30am-5pm.

271
xA5

PAISLEY ABBEY: Paisley town centre, 15km from Glas. Report: 379/OUTSIDE GLASGOW.

BOTHWELL CASTLE, UDDINGSTON: 15km E, via M74. Report: 380/OUTSIDE GLASGOW.

THE BEST WALKS IN THE CITY

See page 10 for walk codes.

272
xA1

KELVIN WALKWAY: A path along the banks of Glasgow's other river, the Kelvin, which enters the Clyde unobtrusively at Yorkhill but first meanders through some of the most interesting parts and parks of the NW city. Walk starts at Kelvingrove Park through the University and Hillhead district under Kelvin Br and on to the celebrated Botanic Grds (263/OTHER ATTRACTIONS). The trail then goes N, under the Forth and Clyde Canal (*see below*) to the Arcadian fields of Dawsholm Park (5km), Killermont (posh golf course) and Kirkintilloch (13km from start). Since the river and the canal shadow each other for much of their routes, it's possible, with a map, to go out by one waterway and return by the other (e.g. start at Gr Western Rd, return Maryhill Rd).

START: Usual start at the Eildon St (off Woodlands Rd) gate of Kelvingrove Park or Kelvin Br. St parking only.

2-13+KM   XCIRC   BIKE   1-A-1

273
D2, C2,
B1

FORTH AND CLYDE CANAL TOWPATH: The canal, opened in 1790 and once a major short cut for fishing boats and trade betw Europe and America, provides a fascinating look round the back of the city from a pathway that stretches on a spur from Pt Dundas just N of the M8 to the main canal at the end of Lochburn Rd off Maryhill Rd and then E all the way to Kirkintilloch and Falkirk, and W through Maryhill and Drumchapel to Bowling and the Clyde (60km). Much of the route is through the forsaken or redeveloped industrial heart of the city, past waste ground, warehouses and high flats, but there are open stretches and curious corners and, by Bishopbriggs, it's a rural waterway. More info from British Waterways (332 6936). Revitalising the whole Edin–Glas link will be a major millennium project.

START: (**1**) Top of Firhill Rd (gr view of city from Ruchill Park, 100m further on, – 278/BEST VIEWS). (**2**) Lochburn Rd (*see above*) at the confluence from which to go E or W to the Clyde. (**3**) Top of Crow Rd, Anniesland where there is a canal side pub, Lock 27 (243/DRINK OUTDOORS), with tables o/side, real ale and food (noon-7/8pm). (**4**) Bishopbriggs Sports Centre, Balmuildy Rd. From here it is 6km to Maryhill and 1km in other direction to the 'country churchyard' of Cadder or 3km to Kirkintilloch. All starts have some parking.

ANY KM   XCIRC   BIKE   1-A-1

POLLOK COUNTRY PARK: The park that (apart from the area around the gallery and the house – 257/MAIN ATTRACTIONS) most feels like a real country park. Numerous trails through woods and meadows. The leisurely Sun guided walks with the park rangers can be educative and more fun than you would think (632 9299). Burrell Collection and Pollok House and Grds are obvious highlights. There's an 'old-fashioned' tearoom in the basement of the latter. Enter by Haggs Rd or by Haggs Castle Golf Course. By car you are directed to the entry rd off Pollokshaws Rd and then to the car park in front of the Burrell. Train to Shawlands or Pollokshaws W from Glas Central Stn.

274
xC5

MUGDOCK COUNTRY PARK: 956 6100. Not perhaps within the city, but one of the nearest and easiest escapes. Park which incl Mugdock Moor, Mugdock Woods (SSSI) and 2 castles is NW of Milngavie. Regular train from Central Stn takes 20mins, then follow route of W Highland Way for 4km across Drumclog Moor to S edge of park. Or take Mugdock Bank bus from stn (not Sat) to end. By car to Milngavie by A81 from Maryhill Rd and left after Black Bull Hotel (on left) and before railway stn (over to rt) up Ellengowan Rd. Continue past reservoir then pick up signs for park. 3 car parks, visitor centre is at second one. Many trails marked out and further afield rambles. This is a godsend betw Glas and the Highland hills.   5-20KM   CAN BE CIRC   BIKE   1-A-2

275
xB1

CATHKIN BRAES: On S edge of city with impressive views. Report: 276/BEST VIEWS.

THE BEST VIEWS OF THE CITY AND BEYOND

276
xC5

CATHKIN BRAES, QUEEN MARY'S SEAT: The southern ridge of the city on the B759 from Carmunnock to Cambuslang, about 12km from centre. Go S of river by Albert Br to Aikenhead Rd which continues S as Carmunnock Rd. Follow to Carmunnock, a delightfully rural village, and pick up the Cathkin Rd. 2km along on the rt is the Cathkin Braes Golf Club and 100m further on the left is the park. Marvellous views to N of the Campsies, Kilpatrick Hills, Ben Lomond and as far as Ben Ledi. Walks on the Braes on both sides of the rd.

277
xB1

QUEEN'S VIEW, AUCHINEDEN: Not so much a view of the city, more a perspective on Glasgow's Highland hinterland, this short walk and sweeping vista to the N has been a Glaswegian pilgrimage for generations. On A809 N from Bearsden about 8km after last r/bout and 2km after the Carbeth Inn which is a v decent pub to repair to. Busy car park attests to its popularity. The walk, along path cut into ridgeside, takes 40-50mins to cairn, from which you can see The Cobbler (393/OUTSIDE GLASGOW), that other Glas favourite, Ben Ledi and sometimes as far as Ben Chonzie 50km away. The fine views of L Lomond are what Queen Victoria came for. Further on is The Whangie (369/WALKS OUTSIDE THE CITY).

1-A-1

278
xC1

RUCHILL PARK: An unlikely but splendid panorama from this overlooked, but well-kept park to the N of the city nr the infamous Possilpark housing estate. Go to top of Firhill Rd (past Partick Thistle football ground) over Forth and Clyde Canal (273/WALKS IN THE CITY) off Garscube Rd where it becomes Maryhill Rd. Best view is from around the flagpole; the whole city among its surrounding hills, from the Campsies to Gleniffer and Cathkin Braes (*see above*), becomes clear.

279
xE2

BAR HILL at TWECHAR, nr KIRKINTILLOCH: 22km N of city, taking A803 Kirkin-tilloch t/off from M8, then the 'low' rd to Kilsyth, the B8023, and bearing lett at the 'black-and-white br'. Next to Twechar Quarry Inn, a path is signed for Bar Hill and the Antonine Wall. Steepish climb for 2km, ignore the strange dome of grass: this isn't it. Over to left in copse of trees are the remains of one of the forts on the wall which stretched across Scotland in the first 2 centuries AD. Ground plan explained on a board. This is a special place with strong history vibes and airy views over the plain to the city which came a long time after.   1-A-2

BLACKHILL, nr LESMAHAGOW: 28km S of city. Another marvellous outlook, but in the opp direction from above. Take jnct 10/11 on M74, then off the B7078 signed Lanark, take the B7018. 4km along past Clarkston Farm, head uphill for 1km and park by Water Board mound. Walk uphill through fields to rt for about 1km. Unprepossessing hill which unexpectedly reveals a vast vista of most of E central Scotland.   1-A-2

280
xE2

PAISLEY ABBEY: About one Sat a month betw May and Oct (1-5pm) on Abbey 'open days', the tower of this amazing edifice can be climbed. The tower (restored 1926) is 50m high and from the top there's a grand view of the Clyde. Obviously this is a rare experience, but phone TO (889 0711) for details; next Sat could be your lucky day. M8 to Paisley; frequent trains from Central Stn. (379/OUTSIDE GLASGOW)

281
xA4

LYLE HILL, GOUROCK: Via M8 W to Greenock, then round the coast to relatively genteel old resort of Gourock where the 'Free French' worked in the yards during the war. A monument has been erected to their memory on the top of Lyle Hill above the town, from where you get one of the most dramatic views of the gr crossroads of the Clyde (Holy L, Gare L and L Long). Best vantage-point is further along the rd on other side by trig pt. Follow British Rail stn signs, then Lyle Hill. There's another gr view of the Clyde further down the water at **HAYLIE, LARGS,** the hill 3km from town reached via the A760 rd to Kilbirnie and Paisley. The island of Cumbrae lies in the sound and the sunset.

282
xA5

CAMPSIE FELLS and **GLENIFFER BRAES**: Reports: 365/366/WALKS OUTSIDE THE CITY.

THE BEST OF THE SPORTS FACILITIES

SWIMMING AND INDOOR SPORTS CENTRES

Well, surprise surprise, the best 2 pools, Arlington Baths (332 6021) and the Western Baths (339 1127), are both private. Temporary memberships may be negotiable. The best of the others are:

283
xE4

WHITEHILL POOL: 551 9969. Onslow Dr parallel to Duke St at Meadowpark St in the E End nr Alexandra Park (phone for times but usually Mon-Fri until 8.30pm and Sat-Sun until 1.45pm). 25m pool with sauna/multigym (Universal).

284
C1

NORTH WOODSIDE LEISURE CENTRE: 332 8102. Braid Sq. Not far from St George's Cross nr Charing Cross at the bottom of Gr Western Rd. In a rebuilt area; follow AA signs. Modern pool (25m) and sauna/steam/sun centre. Open Mon-Fri 8/9am-7/8pm (Sat-Sun 10am-4pm).

285
xC5

POLLOK LEISURE CENTRE: 881 3313. Cowglen Rd. Not a do-your-lengths kind of a pool – more a family water outing. (267/OTHER ATTRACTIONS)

286
xA5

GOUROCK BATHING POOL: 01475 631561. On rd S, an open-air heated pool on the Clyde. Gr prospect for summers like they used to be. (402/OUTSIDE GLASGOW)

287
A2

KELVIN HALL: 357 2525. Argyle St by Kelvingrove Museum and Art Gallery (256/MAIN ATTRACTIONS). Major venue for international indoor sports competitions, but open otherwise for weights/ badminton/tennis/athletics. Book hr-long sessions. No squash.

288
xA2

SCOTSTOUN LEISURE CENTRE: 959 4000. Danes Dr. Huge state-of-the-art sports multiplex. 10 lane pool, indoor halls and outdoor pitches. 9am-10pm, w/ends until 6pm.

289
xE4

MARCO'S: 554 7184. Templeton Business Centre (beside the fabulous Templeton Carpet Factory – 313/ARCHITECTURE), by Glas Green in the E End. Like the Edin one, a labyrinthine and massively successful complex with squash/snooker/gym (Universal and First Class)/indoor jogging track (even though it is next to the Green). Nonmembers OK. 10am-10pm (Sat until 8pm). No pool.

290
xC1

ALLANDER SPORTS CENTRE: 942 2233. Milngavie Rd, Bearsden, 16km N of centre via Maryhill Rd. Best by car. Squash (2 courts) badminton/snooker and swimming pool (open late, but times vary; usually until 10.30 Tue/Thu/Fri and 9pm Sat-Sun). Waiting list for gym.

GOLF COURSES

Glas has a vast number of parks and golf courses. The following clubs are the best of those that are open to nonmembers. Refer to Around Glasgow map on pages 118–19.

CATHKIN BRAES: 634 0650. Cathkin Rd, SE via Aikenhead Rd/Carmunnock Rd to Carmunnock village, then 3km. Best by car. Civilised hilltop course on the v southern edge of the city. Nonmembers Mon-Fri (though probably not Fri am).

291
D3

HAGGS CASTLE: 427 1157. Dumbreck Rd nr jnct 22 of the M8; go straight on to clubhouse at first r/bout. Part of the grounds of Pollok Park; a convenient course, perhaps overplayed, but not difficult to get on.

292
D3

POLLOK GOLF CLUB: 632 1080. On the other side of the White Cart Water and Pollok House and rather more up-market. Well-wooded parkland course, flat and well kept, but not cheap. Women not permitted to play.

293
D3

GLEDDOCH, LANGBANK: 01475 540711. Excellent 18-hole course adj and part of Gleddoch House Hotel (35/HOTELS OUTSIDE TOWN). Restricted play.

294
C3

TENNIS

Public courts (Apr-Sep), membership not required: **KELVINGROVE PARK** 6 courts, **QUEEN'S PARK** 6 courts, **VICTORIA PARK** 6 courts. Courts open 12noon-8pm.

295
B2, xC5, xA2

RIDING

HAZELDEN, NEWTON MEARNS RIDING SCHOOL: 639 3011. A77, 15km SW of city centre.

296
xC5

KENMURE RIDING SCHOOL AND LIVERY YARD: 772 3041. Kenmure Ave, Bishopbriggs, off A803 Kirkintilloch rd. Check opening times.

297
xE2

THE BEST GALLERIES

*Apart from those listed previously (*MAIN ATTRACTIONS, OTHER ATTRAC-
TIONS*) the following galleries are always worth looking into. The* Glasgow
Gallery Guide, *free from any of them, lists all the current exhibs.*

298
D4
✝ ✝ **GLASGOW PRINT STUDIOS:** 552 0704. 22 King St. Influential and accessible upstairs gallery with print work on view and for sale from many of Scotland's leading and rising artists. Cl Sun. Print shop over rd.

299
D4
✝ ✝ **TRANSMISSION GALLERY:** 552 4813. 28 King St. Cutting edge and often off-the-wall work from contemporary Scottish and international artists. Reflects Glasgow's increasing importance as a hot spot of conceptual art. Stuff you might disagree with. Cl Sun-Mon.

300
D3
✝ ✝ **THE GLASGOW ART FAIR:** George Sq in tented pavilions. Held every yr since 1996 in mid-Apr. Most of the galleries on this page and many more (incl rest of Scotland and the UK) are represented; highly selective and good fun. I know a thing or 2 about this event: with Julian Spalding of Glas Museums, I helped to invent it. Do come in 1999.

301
C3
COMPASS GALLERY: 221 6370. 178 W Regent St. Glasgow's oldest established commercial contemporary art gallery. Their 'New Generation' exhib in Jul-Aug shows work from new graduates of the art colleges and has heralded many a career. Combine with the other Gerber gallery (*see below*). Cl Sun.

302
C3
CYRIL GERBER FINE ART: 221 3095. 148 W Regent St. British paintings and esp the Scottish Colourists and 'name' contemporaries. Gerber, the Compass (*see above*), and Art Exposure (*see below*) have Christmas exhibs where small, accessible paintings can be bought for reasonable prices. Cyril will know what's good for you. Cl Sun.

303
E4
ART EXPOSURE GALLERY: 552 7779. 19 Parnie St. Behind the Tron Theatre. Showcase gallery with a friendly, down-to-earth attitude exhibiting the work of contemporary/graduate Scottish artists. Sort of 'affordable'.11am-6pm. Cl Sun.

304
E3
COLLINS GALLERY: 552 4400 (ext 2558). 22 Richmond St. Part of Strathclyde Univ campus (betw George St and Cathedral St). Varied, often important exhibs. Cl Sun.

305
D4
GLASGOW 1999 CENTRE: 227 1999. The Terr, Princes Sq. Excellent, public-access, multi-media exhib space. Work across the spectrum.

THE BEST ARCHITECTURE

The next section is entirely devoted to C.R. Mackintosh (MACKINTOSH) who designed the Glas School of Art, one of the most celebrated buildings, and although he casts a long shadow, his work is only one chapter in the story of Glasgow's architecture.

A short stroll along St Vincent St in a westerly direction, starting from George Sq and returning via Douglas St and finally W George St, will give a good impression of how many quality 19th- and 20th-century buildings there are in Glasgow's city centre. The variety of styles becomes more obvious on closer inspection and the buildings that employ the boldest mixtures of design seem to work the best. Here are the outstanding ones:

BANK OF SCOTLAND: 110-120 St Vincent St. (1927) Architect: James Miller. Monumental neo-classicism, or so I'm told (it's largely Greek to me), but the symmetry, below the huge columns along the front and the tall windows up above, is cleverly designed to make you feel v small.

306
D3

THE HATRACK: 142a-144 St Vincent St. (1899) Architect: James Salmon Jr. Just up the st on the same side is an early example of narrow-frontage design. 10 storeys built on a single house plot with so many windows there's hardly any visible stonework. A v elegant solution to the perennial Scottish problem of lack of natural light.

307
D3

THE ATHENEUM THEATRE: 179 Buchanan St. (1891) Architects: Burnet and Campbell. The inspiration for many buildings and the first of its kind in Glas. With a strange, narrow, asymmetrical frontage studded with arch and bay windows on one side and curious arrow-slits on the other, decorated with statuary and topped with an octagonal cupola, all vying for attention but somehow creating an eccentric, and typically Glaswegian, whole.

308
D3

THE PEARCE INSTITUTE: 840 Govan Rd. (1903) Architect: Sir Rowand Anderson. Commissioned by shipbuilders, this is another example of eclectic design. The main façade is in the style of a 17th-century town building but where the eastern end is almost severe, the western end is flamboyantly Renaissance in character, with its curvaceous gable and detailed, heraldic sculpture over the huge mullioned window. Built at a time when, according to Anderson, architecture in Scotland was 'in a more vigorous and healthy state than in any other country in Europe'.

309
xA4

310
C4

SCOTTISH COOPERATIVE: 95 Morrison St. (1897) Architects: Bruce and Hay. Just a big warehouse really, but when you're skimming past in your car, level with the top floor, on the S-side slip rd off the Kingston Br, all of a sudden it becomes Gotham City . . . and at the other end of the br, on the city-bound off ramp, you get the futuristic equivalent, gliding down between the twin glass mono-liths of the **EAGLE BUILDING** (1990, Keppie Design) and the former **BRIT-OIL BUILDING** (1988, Hugh Martin), to land at the foot of Alexander Thomson's spectacular **ST VINCENT ST CHURCH** set on a massive plinth on the corner of Pitt St and St Vincent St. Awarded 'World Monument' status in 1997. (Rumour has it that this is the church setting used in Ian Banks' *Espedair St.*)

311
B2, A2

At the beginning of Woodlands Terr there's a flight of 1850s moss-clad, stone steps that lead down into Kelvingrove Park on the rt. By following the path up to the Bruce monument you can take in the High Victorian sweep of **PARK CIRCUS** and then the view of Gilmorehill with **GLASGOW UNIVERSITY** (1870, Sir George Gilbert Scott and son John Oldrid Scott), at the top, with its towering spire and vaulted passageways, and the **ART GALLERY/MUSEUM** (1900, Sir J.W. Simpson and Milner Allen), massive and grandiose, at the foot, separated by the R Kelvin (256/MAIN ATTRACTIONS).

312
A4, A3

Although it's a work of engineering, and therefore doesn't strictly belong here, **THE CLYDE NAVIGATION TRUST'S CRANE NO. 7**, better known as the 'Finnieston Cran', stands as a poignant reminder of Glasgow's maritime past and the many thousands of people who worked here in the shipyards. Perhaps one day you'll be able to sail up the Clyde again, and as you do you'll see the 'Cran' and beside it, the **GLASGOW CONFERENCE CENTRE** itself, also better known as the 'Armadillo', and you'll know you're nearing jour-ney's end, the heart of Glas.

313
xE5

TEMPLETON'S CARPET FACTORY: Glas Green. Last, but not least. Where one can truly state, 'They don't build them like that any-more.'

THE MACKINTOSH TRAIL

The gr Scottish architect and designer Charles Rennie Mackintosh (1868-1928) had an extraordinary influence on contemporary design. Glas is the best place to see his work.

✠ ✠ ✠ **GLASGOW SCHOOL OF ART:** 353 4500. 167 Renfrew St. Mackintosh's supreme architectural triumph. It's enough almost to admire it from the st (and maybe best, since this is v much a working college) but there are guided tours at 11am and 2pm (Sat 10.30am) of the sombre yet light interior, the halls and library. You might wonder if the building itself could be partly responsible for it's remarkable output of acclaimed painters. The Tenement House (266/OTHER ATTRACTIONS) is nearby.

314
C3

✠ ✠ **QUEEN'S CROSS CHURCH:** 870 Garscube Rd, where it becomes Maryhill Rd (corner of Springbank St). Built 1896-99. Calm and simple, the antithesis of Victorian Gothic. If all churches had been built like this, we'd go more often. The HQ of the Charles Rennie Mackintosh Society, which was founded in 1973 (phone 946 6600). Mon-Fri 10.30am-5.00pm, Sun 2.30am-5pm. FREE

315
xC1

✠ ✠ **MACKINTOSH HOUSE:** 330 5431. Univ Ave. Opp and part of the Hunterian Museum (261/MAIN ATTRACTIONS) within the univ campus. The Master's house has been transplanted and methodically reconstructed from the next st (they say even the light is the same). If you've ever wondered what the fuss is about, go and see how innovative and complete an artist, designer and architect he was, in this inspiring yet habitable set of rms. Mon-Sat 9.30am-5pm (cl 12.30-1.30pm). FREE

316
A1

✠ ✠ **SCOTLAND STREET SCHOOL:** 429 1202. 225 Scotland St. Opp Shields Rd underground and best app by car from Eglinton St (A77 Kilmarnock Rd over Jamaica St Br). Entire school (from 1906) preserved as museum of education through Victorian/Edwardian and wartimes. Original, exquisite Mackintosh features, esp tiling, and powerfully redolent of happy school days. This is a uniquely evocative time capsule. Café and temporary exhibs. Mon-Sat 10am-5pm, Sun 2-5pm. FREE

317
B5

WILLOW TEAROOM: Sauchiehall St. The café he designed (or what's left of it); certainly where to go for a tea break on the trail (145/BEST TEAROOMS).

318
D3

319
AROUND
GLASGOW
C3

THE HILL HOUSE, HELENSBURGH: 01436 673900. Upper Colquhoun St. Take Sinclair St off Princes St (at Romanesque tower and TO) and go 2km uphill, taking left at Kennedy Dr and follow signs. A complete house incorporating Mackintosh's typical total unity of design, built for Walter Blackie in 1902-4. Much to marvel over and wish that everybody else would go away and you could stay there for the night. There's even a library full of books to keep you occupied. Tearoom; grds. Open Apr-Dec 1.30-5.30pm. Helensburgh is 45km NW of city centre via Dumbarton (A82) and A814 up N Clyde coast.   ADMN

320
xA5

HOUSE FOR AN ART LOVER: 353 4770. Bellahouston Park. 10 Dumbreck Rd. Take the M8 W, then the M77, turn rt onto Dumbreck Rd and it's on your left. These rms were designed, nearly a century ago, specifically, it would seem, for willowy women to come and go, talking of Michelangelo. Detail is the essence of Mackintosh, and there's plenty here, but the overall effect is of space and light and a complete absence of clutter. Design shop and Exhibition Café (147/BEST TEAROOMS, 165/COFFEE) on the ground floor. Daily 10am-5pm.   ADMN

GLASGOW SCHOOL OF ART 'Mackintosh's supreme architectural triumph' (page 93)

GOOD NIGHTLIFE

For the current programmes of the places below and all other venues, consult The List *magazine, on sale fortnightly at most newsagents.*

CINEMA

There are all the usual multiplexes, but the best picture houses are:

321
C3

GLASGOW FILM THEATRE: 332 6535. Rose St at downtown end of Sauchiehall St. Known affectionately as GFT, has bar and 2 screens for essential art house flicks.

322
A1

GROSVENOR: 339 4928. Ashton Lane, off Byres Rd behind Hillhead Stn. Busy lane for eats and nightlife as well as this old cinema with 2 screens and a selected programme of mainly current hits.

THEATRE

323
D5

✠ ✠ **THE CITIZENS':** 429 0022. Gorbals St, just over the river. Fabulous main auditorium and 2 small studios. Drama at its v best. One of Britain's most influential theatres, especially for design. Reopened after lottery-funded renovations, now ready to take on the world – the one we love.

324
xC5

✠ ✠ **THE TRAMWAY:** 422 2023. 25 Albert Dr on S-side. A theatre and vast performance space. Dynamic and widely influential with an innovative and varied programme from all over the world. Seasonal programme.

325
C3

✠ **CCA:** 332 7521. Centre for Contemporary Arts, 350 Sauchiehall St. Central arts-lab complex, notable as a theatre for modern dance (esp in spring with its New Moves programme), but also has gallery and other performance space and a good café (152/BEST TEAROOMS). Cl Sun.

326
D4

✠ **THE ARCHES:** 221 9736. Midland St, betw Jamaica St and Oswald St. Experimental and vital theatre on a tight budget in the railway arches under the tracks of Central Stn. Andy Arnold will not lie down. Opening times vary. W/end clubs among the best (357/CLUBS).

327
D3

RSAMD: 332 4101. 100 Renfrew St. The Royal Scottish Academy of Music and Drama. Part and wholly student productions often with guest directors. Eclectic, often powerful mix.

THE TRON THEATRE: 552 4267. 63 Trongate. Contemporary Scottish theatre and other interesting performance, esp music. Recent face-lift. Gr café-bar with food before and *après* (70/BEST BISTROS).

328
E4

KING'S THEATRE: 227 5511. Bath St. Trad theatre with shows like pantos, Gilbert and Sullivan and major touring musicals.

329
C3

CLASSICAL MUSIC

THEATRE ROYAL: 332 3321. Hope St. Home of Scottish Opera, with a mainly high-brow diet of opera, ballet (from Scottish Ballet) and some drama.

330
D3

GLASGOW ROYAL CONCERT HALL: 332 6633. Top of Buchanan St. Sep-Apr subscription series and Jun Proms from the Royal Scottish National Orchestra, plus visits from national and international orchestras.

331
D3

CITY HALLS: 227 5511. Candleriggs. Winter subscription series provided by the Scottish Chamber Orchestra and BBC Scottish Symphony Orchestra.

332
E4

RSAMD: 332 4101. 110 Renfrew St. Student concerts plus recitals from visiting ensembles and artistes.

333
D3

HUTCHESON'S HALL: 552 8391. 158 Ingram St. Chamber concerts and recitals in this NTS property.

334
E4

JAZZ

335

For residencies and one-offs, see *The List* or *Live Scene,* a monthly freesheet available at most music pubs and venues. The most consistent and coherent programme is in the **INTERNATIONAL JAZZ FESTIVAL** in early Jul (227 5511). Most frequently used venues during rest of yr are **THE BABY GRAND**, **THE TAP** and **BLACKFRIARS**. Sun afternoon jazz upstairs at the **PAISLEY ARTS CENTRE**, New St (887 1010). Occasional performances at **PIZZA EXPRESS**, 151 Queen St (221 3333), and concerts at the **MITCHELL THEATRE** (287 4855).

THE BEST FOLK MUSIC AND CEILIDHS

336
D3

✠ **GLASGOW ROYAL CONCERT HALL, CELTIC CONNECTIONS:** 332 6633. Major jamboree every Jan. 3 weeks of concerts, ceilidhs and gatherings. Broad appeal.

337
D4

CLUTHA VAULTS: 167 Stockwell St. E end nr Clyde. Gr atmos for the drink and the music. Mixed programme: readings Tue, blue-grass Sat afternoons. (194/GREAT GLAS PUBS)

338
A2

THE HALT BAR: Woodlands Rd. Among a mixed music programme, always some folk for the kind of folk who inhabit the bar (197/GREAT GLAS PUBS). Wed.

339
D4

SCOTIA BAR: 112 Stockwell St. The folk club and writers' retreat and all things non-high cultural. Club meets Wed night and Sat afternoons. Always the 'right folk' here. (193/GREAT GLAS PUBS)

340
D4

VICTORIA BAR: Bridgegate. Nr the Scotia (*see above*) and a similar set-up. Fri and Sat night sessions of Irish/Scottish trad music.. (192/GREAT GLAS PUBS)

341
C4

THE RENFREW FERRY: Enter by Clyde Pl via Jamaica St Br from N of river or Br St. A real ferry moored on the Clyde – brilliant ambience for ceilidhs and gigs of all kinds. Fri 9pm-2am. Tickets at quay or in advance from Ticket Centre, Candleriggs (227 5511), usually sold out by 10pm. Visitors and locals. Gr bands.

342
D4

THE RIVERSIDE: 248 3144. Fox St, off Clyde St. The place that start-ed the ceilidh revival in Glas. Upstairs in quiet st, the joint is jump-ing. Fri-Sat from 8pm, fills up quickly. Good bands. Good, mixed crowd.

THE BEST ROCK AND POP MUSIC

For live music in smaller venues, see PUBS AND CLUBS WITH GOOD LIVE MUSIC.

♰ ♰ ♰ **BARROWLAND BALLROOM:** Gallowgate. When its lights are on, you can't miss it. The Barrowland is world-famous and for many bands one of their favourite gigs. It's tacky and a bit run-down, but distinctly venerable; and with its high stage and sprung dance floor, perfect for rock 'n' roll. The Glas audience is one of the best in the world and many tours begin here to pick up on the special atmos. We love it 'live'.

343
xE4

SECC: 248 3000. Finnieston Quay beyond the city centre and, for many, beyond the pale as far as concerts are concerned (big shed, not big on atmos), but there are 3 different-sized halls for mainly arena-sized acts and everyone from Eric to Pav and Oasis have played here. Glasgow's own, Wet Wet Wet, currently hold the record for numbers of nights sold.

344
A3

Neither of the above venues has its own box office. For tickets and information check with Tower Records, Argyle St, 204 2500 and Virgin Records, Argyle St, 204 5151, and for credit card bookings 227 5511.

PAVILION THEATRE: 332 1846. Renfield St. Regular concerts and a cosier place to watch a band.

345
D3

GAY GLASGOW THE BEST!

Big improvements of late, the scene developing in the Merchant City around Virginia St/Wilson St nr Bennets. In Glas, many bars close at 12midnight, but may open until 1am at w/ends.

346
D4

♣ DELMONICA'S: 552 4803. 68 Virginia St. Newly refurbed stylish pub with long bar and open plan in quiet lane in Merchant City. Food until 7pm. Pally, pre-club crowd later on. Some event nights. 7 days until 12midnight.

347
D4

♣ POLO LOUNGE: 553 1221. 84 Wilson St. Classiest Glas gay bar yet by same people who own Delmonica's (*see above*) and Caffe Latte (*see below*). Comfortable and clubbable by day, cruisier by night. Downstairs disco (Fri-Sun) with 3am licence; otherwise until 1am. (240/THESE ARE HIP)

348
D3

AUSTINS: 332 2707. 183a Hope St. Downstairs bar in busy central st out of zone. Older chaps and young friends. More mixed in daytime. 7 days until 1am.

349
C3

WATERLOO BAR: 221 7539. 306 Argyle St. Old-established bar and clientele. Not really for trendy young things. You might not fancy anybody but they're a friendly down-to-earth old bunch. 7 days until 12midnight.

350
C3

SQUIRE'S LOUNGE: 221 9184. 106 W Campbell St. Below st level; not exactly a dive bar but small and can be cruisy. This bar has an agreeable anonymity – you could be anywhere in the W (west of the world). Mixed ages. Trashy music. 7 days until 12midnight.

351
D3

SADIE FROSTS: 332 8005. 8 W George St, in front of Queen St Stn and underneath Burger King. Downtown cruisy bar, well placed for the brief encounter. Gets jumpy nr closing time (12midnight, 7 days). **SAPPHO'S:** Glasgow's all-women bar is also here. All kinds of gals. Pool table. Tue-Sun 7pm-12midnight.

352
D4

BENNETS: 552 5761. 80 Glassford St. For 20yrs the real disco. Everybody goes in the beginning – and in the end. Recent face-lift, so she's looking good again. Wed-Sun 11pm-3am, Tue is 'traditionally' straight night.

OTHER PLACES

CAFFE LATTE: 553 2553. Corner of Virginia St and Wilson St. Recently opened café-bistro at heart of gay st; antithesis of the gay bar. Laid-back atmos; snacks and food all day until 12midnight. (167/COFFEE)

353
D4

CLONE ZONE: 552 3103. As in London, shop for mags, videos and things to play with. 7 days until 6pm (Thu-Sat until 10pm, Sun until 7pm).

354
D4

CENTURION SAUNA: 248 4485. 19 Dixon St, above Aer Lingus. Uncomfortable layout. As saunas go, low on cruiseability. Until 10pm or later.

355
D4

HOTEL

ALBION HOTEL: 339 8620. 405 N Woodside Rd, off Gr Western Rd. Currently Glasgow's only prospect is gay-friendly (i.e. they advertise in *Gay Times*) rather than gay. It's a start.

356
B1

16RMS   JAN-DEC   T/T   PETS   CC   KIDS   MED.INX

THE BEST CLUBS

Many of the best clubs come and go and there's little point in mentioning them here. Some are only on once a week with no permanent venue. Consult The List (fortnightly) for up-to-date info, and look for flyers. Glas is a club city, but the dreaded curfew remains – check the following for current 'rules'.

357
D4

CLUBS AT THE ARCHES: 221 9736. At the Arches Theatre, Midland St (326/NIGHTLIFE), w/ends only. Glasgow's finest. 2/3 vaulted archways, serious sound system and v up-for-it crowd. Best clubs: Cool Lemon, Love Boutique, Colours.

358
D4

ARCHAOS: 204 3189. 25 Queen St. Huge dance emporium on 3 floors, incl Betty's Mayonnaise. Central dance floor has state-of-the-art lighting. Balconies upstairs for action-checking and chilling. Atmos more rarified the higher you go.

359
D4

THE TUNNEL: 204 1000. 84 Mitchell St. Once defined club culture in Glas. Still high-glam quotient and designer ambience with vogue-ish crowd. W/ends (Ark and Triumph) and student nights. On same circuit as Liverpool's Cream so big-name DJs every month.

360
D4

THE APARTMENT: 221 7080. 23 Royal Exchange Sq. Colin and Kelly Barr's stylish drinking club kind of disco for older more discerning types. Exclusivity is part of the deal, but they have been known to let in any old footballer and hairdresser. Usually have their finger on the pulse and the rt guest lists, so whatever they're up to next is probably cool. Open Thu-Mon from 11pm.

361
D4

TIN PAN ALLEY: 248 8832. Mitchell St. Spacious clubland over 3 floors and many yrs. Good for new talent (DJs, that is) on certain nights, otherwise mainstream.

362
D4

THE SUB CLUB: 248 4600. 22 Jamaica St. Long-running, but revamped and still v much a scene. Eclectic music policy. Fri-Sat (some Thu and Sun).

363
C3

REDS: Upstairs at Nico's, 379 Sauchiehall St. Safe, studenty. Not so bad. W/ends.

364
C3

THE GARAGE: 332 1120. 490 Sauchiehall St. The big night out for cheap drinks, chart sounds and copping off. Totally unpretentious. Live bands as advertised.

TEMPLETON'S CARPET FACTORY 'They don't build them like that anymore' (page 92)

BOTANIC GARDENS AND KIBBLE PALACE 'a wonderful place to muse and wander' (page 81)

WHERE TO GO OUT OF TOWN

EASY WALKS OUTSIDE THE CITY

See page 10 for walk codes. Refer to Around Glasgow map on pages 118–19.

365
D3

CAMPSIE FELLS: Range of hills 25km N of city best reached via Kirkintilloch or Cumbernauld/Kilsyth. Encompasses area that includes the Kilsyth Hills, Fintry Hills and Carron Valley betw. (**1**) Good app from A803, Kilsyth main st up the Tak-me-Doon (*sic*) rd. Park by the golf club and follow path by the burn. It's poss to take in the two hills to left as well as Tomtain (453m), the most easterly of the tops, in a good afternoon; views to the E. (**2**) Drive on to the jnct (9km) of the B818 rd to Fintry and go left, following Carron Valley reservoir to the far corner where there is a forestry rd to the left. Park here and follow track to ascend Meikle Bin (570m) to the rt, the highest peak in the central Campsies. (**3**) The bonny village of Fintry (HOTELS OUTSIDE TOWN) is a good start/base for the Fintry Hills and Earl's Seat (578m).

10KM+   CAN BE CIRC   XBIKE   2-B-2

366
D3

GLENIFFER BRAES, PAISLEY: Ridge to the S of Paisley (15km from Glas) has been a favourite walking-place for centuries. M8 or Paisley Rd W to town centre then: (**1**) S via B775/A736 towards Irvine or (**2**) B774 (Causewayside then Neilston Rd) and sharp rt after 3km to Glenfield Rd (Bus: Clydeside 24). For (**1**) go 2km after last houses, winding up ridge and park/start at Robertson Park (signed). Here there are superb views and walks marked to E and W. (**2**) 500m along Glenfield Rd is a car park/ranger centre. Walk up through grds and formal parkland and then W along marked paths and trails. Eventually, after 5km, this route joins (**1**).

2-10KM   CAN BE CIRC   MTBIKE   1-A-2

367
C3

GREENOCK CUT: 45km W of Glas. Can app via Pt Glas but simplest route is from A78 rd to Largs. Travelling S from Pt Glas take first left after IBM, signed L Thom. Lochside 5km up winding rd. Park at Cornalees Br Centre. Walk left along lochside rd to Overton (5km) then path is signed. The Cut, an aqueduct built in 1827 to supply water to Greenock and its 31 mills, is now an ancient monument. Gr views from the mast over the Clyde. Another route to the rt from Cornalees leads through a glen of birch, rowan and oak to the Kelly Cut. Both trails described on board at the car park.

15/16KM   CIRC   MTBIKE   1-B-2

368
C3

MUIRSHIEL: General name for vast area of 'Inverclyde' W of city, incl Greenock Cut (*see above*), Castle Semple Country Park and Lunderston Bay, a stretch of coastline nr the Cloch Lighthouse on the A770 S of Gourock for littoral amblings. But best wildish bit is Muirshiel Country Park itself, with trails, a waterfall and Windy Hill (350m). Nothing arduous, but a breath of air. From Pt Glas head S on A761 for Kilmalcolm then S for Lochwinnoch on B786.

THE WHANGIE: On A809 N from Bearsden about 8km after last r/bout and 2km after the Carbeth Inn, is the car park for the Queen's View (277/BEST VIEWS). Climb uphill towards the stand of conifers and over the stile. Of 2 paths, one leads along the top of the scarp, while the other lower down runs parallel to it and offers more protection from the elements. Both lead to the westerly end of the escarpment. Once you get to the summit of Auchineden Hill, take the path that drops down to the W (a half-rt-angle) and look for crags on your rt. This is the 'back door' of The Whangie. The path then seems to disappear into the side of the hill but carry on and you'll suddenly find yourself in a deep cleft in the rock face with sheer walls rising over 10m on either side. The Whangie is more than 100m long and at one pt the walls narrow to less than 1m. As you emerge, take the lowest path, back along the face of the hill to the stile and then down to the car park. Local mythology has it that The Whangie was made by The Devil, who lashed his tail in anticipation of a witchy rendezvous somewhere in the N, and carved a slice through the rock, where the path now goes.

5KM   CIRC   XBIKE   XDOGS   1-A-1

369
D3

CHATELHÉRAULT, nr HAMILTON: Jnct 6 off M74, well signposted into Hamilton, follow rd into centre, then bear left away from main rd where it's signed for A723. The gates to the 'château' are about 3km o/side town. A drive leads to the William Adam-designed hunting lodge of the Dukes of Hamilton, set amid ornamental grds with a notable parterre and extensive grounds. Tracks along the deep, wooded glen of the Avon (ruins of Cadzow Castle) lead to distant glades. Ranger service and good guided walks (01698 426213). 20km SE of city centre. House open 10.30am-4.30pm, walks at all times.   2-7KM   CIRC   BIKE   1-A-2

370
D3

WHERE TO TAKE KIDS

Refer to Around Glasgow map on pages 118–19.

371
C4

✚ **KIDZ PLAY, PRESTWICK:** 01292 475215. Off main st at Stn Rd, past stn to beach and to rt. Big shed that's a soft play area for kids. Everything that the little blighters will like in the throwing-themselves-around department. Shriek city and a non-parent nightmare zone. They never had anything like this in my day, only trees (he said, Day-Glo green with envy). 7 days, 9.30am-7pm.

372
C3

KELBURN COUNTRY CENTRE, LARGS: 2km S of Largs on A78. Riding school, grds, woodland walks up the Kel Burn and a central visitor/consumer section with shops/exhibs/cafés. Wooden stockade for clambering kids; commando assault course for exhibitionist adults and less doddering dads. Falconry displays (and long-suffering owl). Kelburn continues to develop its range of attractions: a Secret Forest has appeared in the woods. Combine with Vikingar! (*see below*) for an exhausting day. Stock up with chips and Nardini's ice cream (412/OUTSIDE GLASGOW). 7 days, 10am-6pm.

373
D4

LOUDON CASTLE, nr GALSTON: Recent theme park in S of Glas hinterland. Just off A71 Kilmarnock–Edin rd (go from Glas via A77 Kilmarnock rd). Behind the ruins of the said Loudon Castle (burned out in 1941) a fairground which incl the 'largest carousel in Europe' and massive 'chairy-plane' has been transplanted in the old walled gdn. Nice setting: well, kids might not notice the setting, but they won't forget the chairy plane. Open AYR, 10am-dusk.

374
E3

PALACERIGG COUNTRY PARK, CUMBERNAULD: 01236 720047. 6km E of Cumbernauld. 740 acres of parkland; ranger service, nature trails, picnic area and kids' farm. 18-hole golf course and putting green. Exhib area with changing exhibs about forestry, convservation, etc. Open AYR daylight hrs. Visitor centre and tearoom until 6.30pm summer, 4.30pm winter.

375
E3

THE TIME CAPSULE, MONKLANDS: 01236 449572. They say Monklands, but where you are going is downtown Coatbridge, about 15km from Glas via the M8. Known rather meanly as the 'Tim Capture' (local joke – you don't want to know!). Essentially a leisure (rather than a swimming) pool and ice rink lavishly fitted out on prehistoric monster theme. Even if you haven't been swimming for yrs, this is the sort of place you force the flab into the swimsuit. Cafés and view areas. Facs of the clean-up-your-act variety (e.g. squash, sauna, sun, steam, gym). 'Courses'. 10am-10pm.

VIKINGAR!, LARGS: Suddenly fulfilled all the needs and gaps in this busy visitor area of the Clyde coast – a pool and sports centre, a theatre, an indoor attraction and a dab of heritage. Got the award. But hey . . . it works. It won't exercise your intellect, but the other bits will do just fine. 7 days, 10.30am-6pm (until 4pm in winter).

376
C3

DOLLAN AQUA CENTRE, TOWN CENTRE PARK, EAST KILBRIDE: 01355 260000. EK: The 'Gr Experiment' in New Town planning, which just celebrated its 50th birthday, now boasts a quality leisure centre. 50m pool, fitness facs, soft play area and Scotland's first interactive flume (aquatic pinball machine with you as the ball – there had to be a twist!). Mon-Wed 7.30am-10pm, Thu-Fri 8am-10pm, Sat-Sun 8am-6pm. Last sessions 2hrs before closing.

377
D3

BEST PLACES OUTSIDE GLASGOW

Refer to Around Glasgow map on pages 118–19.

HISTORICAL PLACES

378
C4

✝ ✝ **CULZEAN CASTLE, MAYBOLE:** 24km S of Ayr on A719. Impossible to convey here the scale and the scope of the house and country park. Allow some hrs esp for the grounds. Castle is more like a country house and you examine from other side of a rope. From the 12th century but rebuilt by Robert Adam in 1775, a time of soaring ambition, its grandeur is almost out of place in this exposed clifftop position. It was designed for entertaining and the oval staircase is magnificent. Wartime associations (esp with President Eisenhower, which will interest Americans), plus the enduring fascination of the aristocracy. 560 acres of grounds, incl clifftop walk, formal grds, walled grd, Swan Pond (a must) and Happy Valley. Harmonious home farm is a visitor centre with café, exhibs, shop, etc. Apr-Oct 10am-5pm. Culzean is pronounced 'Cullane'.

379
D3

✝ ✝ **PAISLEY ABBEY:** Town centre. An abbey founded in 1163, razed by the English in 1307 and with successive deteriorations and renovations ever since. Major restoration in the 1920s brought it to present-day cathedral-like magnificence. Exceptional stained glass (the recent window complementing the formidable Strachan E Window), an impressive choir and an edifying sense of space. Sun services (11am and 6.30pm) are superb, esp full-dress communion, and there are open days (about one Sat a month, phone TO 889 0711) with coffee in the cloisters, organ music and the tower open for climbing. Otherwise abbey open AYR 10am-3.30pm. Café/shop. (281/BEST VIEWS)

380
D3

BOTHWELL CASTLE, UDDINGSTON: 15km E of Glas via M74, Uddingston t/off into main st and follow signs. Hugely impressive 13th-century ruin, the home of the Black Douglases, o/looking the Clyde. Remarkable considering proximity to city that there is hardly any 20th-century intrusion except yourself. Pay to go inside. Walk down to Clyde and enjoy riverside trails to Blantyre.

381
D3

HAMILTON MAUSOLEUM, STRATHCLYDE PARK: Off (and visible from) M74 at jnct 5/6, 15km from Glas. Huge over-the-top/over-the-tomb (though removed 1921) stone memorial to the 10th Duke of Hamilton. Guided tours daily (Easter-Sep at 3pm and, even better, evenings in Jul and Aug at 7pm; winter Sat-Sun at 3pm). Eerie and chilling and with remarkable acoustics – the 'longest echo in Europe'. Give it a shout or take your violin.

CROSSRAGUEL ABBEY, MAYBOLE: 24km S of Ayr on A77. Built 1244, one of the first Cluniac settlements in Scotland, an influential and rich order, stripped in the Reformation. Now an extensive ruin of architectural distinction, the ground plan is v well preserved and obvious. Open daily.

382
C4

CHATELHÉRAULT, nr HAMILTON: Report: 370/WALKS OUTSIDE THE CITY.

OUTDOOR PLACES

✝ ✝ **THE YOUNGER BOTANIC GARDEN, BENMORE:** 12km from Dunoon on the A815 to Strachur. An 'outstation' of the Royal Botanic in Edin, gifted to the nation by Harry the Younger in 1928, but the first plantations dating from 1820. Walks clearly marked through formal grds, woody grounds and the 'pinetum' where the air is so sweet and spicy it can seem like the v elixir of life. Redwood ave, terr hillsides, views; a grd of different moods and fine proportions. Café. Apr-Oct 10am-6pm.   ADM

383
C3

✝ ✝ **ROTHESAY–TIGNABRUAICH:** A886/A8003. The most celebrated part of this route is the latter, the A8003 down the side of L Riddon to Tignabruaich along the hillsides which give the breathtaking views of Bute and the Kyles, but the whole way, with its diverse aspects of lochside, riverine and rocky scenery, is supernatural. Incl short ferry crossing between Rhubodach and Colintraive.

384
C3

✝ **OSTAL BEACH/KILBRIDE BAY, MILLHOUSE, nr TIGNABRUAICH:** Down rd from 'Millhouse corner' on B8000, a track to the rt at a white house (there's a church on the left) marked 'Private road, no cars' (often with a chain across to restrict access). Park and walk 1km, turning rt after lochan. You arrive on a perfect white sandy cres known locally as Ostal and, apart from stranded jellyfish and the odd swatch of sewage, in certain conditions, a mystical secret place to swim and picnic. The N coast of Arran is like a Greek island in the bay.

385
C3

FALLS OF CLYDE, NEW LANARK: Dramatic falls in a long gorge of the Clyde. New Lanark, the conservation village of Robert Owen the social reformer, is signed from Lanark. It's hard to avoid the

386
E3

'award-winning' tourist bazaar, but I'd recommend getting out of the village and along the riverbank ASAP. The path to the power stn is about 3km, but the route doesn't get interesting until after it, a 1km climb to the first fall (Cora Linn) and another 1km to the next (Bonnington Linn). Swimming above or below them is not advised (but it's gr). Certainly don't swim on an 'open day', when they close the stn and divert all the water back down the river in a mighty surge (about once a month in summer on Sun, phone TO 01555 661661).

387
E3
STRATHCLYDE PARK, betw HAMILTON AND MOTHERWELL: 15km SE of Glas. Take M8/A725 interchange or M74 jnct 5 or 6. Scotland's most popular country park, esp for watersports on the 'man-made' lake. Everything from canoeing to parascending and you can hire all the gear there. Also excavated Roman bath house, play-grounds, sports pitches and now that the trees are beginning to mature, some pleasant walks too. Also Hamilton Mausoleum (*see above*). Nearby Baron's Haugh and Dalzell Country Park more notable for their nature trails and grds. (30/CAMPING)

388
C3
LOCHWINNOCH: 30km SW of Glas via M8 jnct 29 then A737 and A760 past Johnstone. Also from Largs 20km via A760. A nature reserve just o/side the village on lochside and comprising wetland and woodland habitats. A serious 'nature centre' incorporating an observation tower. Hides and marked trails; and a birds-spotted board. Shop and coffee shop. Good for kids. Centre 10am-5pm. (31/CAMPING)

389
C4
EGLINTON COUNTRY PARK, nr IRVINE: Beside main A78 Largs–Ayr rd signed from Irvine/Kilwinning intersection. Spacious lungful of Ayrshire nr new town nexus and traffic tribulations. Visitor centre with interpretation of absolutely everything; network of walks. Not much left of the house. A factory makes 'ambient foods'. All a bit of a construct, but some parts are peaceful.

390
D2
CONIC HILL, BALMAHA, L LOMOND: An easier climb than the Ben up the rd (*see below*) and a good place to view it from, Conic, on the Highland fault line, is one of the first Highland hills you reach from Glas. Stunning views also of L Lomond from its 358m peak. Ascend through woodland from the corner of Balmaha car park. Watch for buzzards and your footing on the final crumbly bits. 1.5hr up. 2-A-2

BEN LOMOND, ROWARDENNAN, L LOMOND: Many folk's first Munro, given proximity to Glas (soul and city). It's not too taxing a climb Munro-wise and has rewarding views (in good weather). 2 main ascents: 'tourist route' is easier, from toilet block at Rowardennan car park (end of rd from Drymen), well trodden all the way; or 500m up past youth hostel, a path follows burn – the 'Ptarmigan route'. Circular walk possible. 3hrs up.

391
D2

2-A-2

TINTO HILL, betw BIGGAR AND LANARK: A favourite climb in S/Central Scotland with easy access to start from A73 nr Symington, 10km S of Lanark. Park 100m behind Tinto Hills farm shop, after stocking up with rolls and juice. Good track, though it has its ups and downs before you get there. Braw views. 707m. Allow 3hrs.

392
E4

2-A-2

THE COBBLER (BEN ARTHUR), ARROCHAR: Perennial favourite of the Glas hill walker and, for sheer exhilaration, the most popular of 'the Arrochar Alps'. A motorway path ascends from the A83 on the other side of L Long from Arrochar (park in the new car park at the head of the loch) and it takes 2.5-3hrs to traverse the up 'n' down route to the top. Just short of a Munro at 881m, it has 3 tops, of which the N peak is the simplest scramble (central and S peaks for climbers). Way isn't marked; consult map or other walkers.

393
C2

2-B-3

ACTIVITY PLACES

TURNBERRY: 01655 331000. Ailsa (championship) and Arran. Sometimes poss by application. Otherwise you must stay at the hotel. Superb.

394
C4

ROYAL OLD COURSE, TROON: V difficult to get on. No wimmen. Staying at Marine Highland Hotel (01292 314444) helps. Easier is **THE PORTLAND COURSE**: across rd from Royal. Both 01292 311555.

395
C4

GLASGOW GAILES/WESTERN GAILES: 01294 311347/311649. Superb links courses next to one another, 5km S of Irvine off the A78.

396
C4

OLD PRESTWICK: 01292 477404. Original home of the Open and 'every challenge you'd wish to meet'. Hotels opp (e.g. the Golf View, 01292 671234) cost less than a round. Unlikely to get on at w/ends.

397
C4

398
C4

BELLEISLE, AYR: 01292 441258. Good parkland course. Easy to get on.

399
C3

ROTHESAY: 01700 503554. Sloping golf course with breathtaking views of Clyde. Visitors welcome. What could be finer than taking the train from Glas to Wemyss Bay for the ferry over and 18 holes. Finish up with fish 'n' chips at The W End on the way home.

400
D2

L LOMOND GOLF COURSE, LUSS: On A82 1km from conservation village of Luss. Exclusive American-owned club; membership only 5000 bucks! We can buy a cheaper season ticket to see the annual World Invitational tournament (early Jul; tickets 0990 661661); but no access to plebs to clubhouse. 18 holes of scenic golf by the loch, with Jack Nicklaus due to design additional course soon. This is golfing for gold.

401
C3

KIP MARINA, INVERKIP: 01475 521485. Major sailing centre on Clyde coast 50km W of Glas via M8, A8 and A78 from Pt Glas heading S for Largs. A yacht heaven as well as haven of Grand Prix status. Sails, charters, pub/restau, chandlers and myriad boats. Diving equipment, jet skis and dinghies for hire.

402
C3

✠ **GOUROCK BATHING POOL:** 01475 315611. One of only 2 remaining (proper) open-air pools in Scotland that are still open. On coast rd S of town centre 45km from central Glas. 1950s style leisure. Heated, so it doesn't need to be a scorcher (brilliant, but crowded when it is). Open 'in season' 10am-8pm, Sun until 5pm.

403
E3

✠ **STRATHCLYDE PARK WATERSPORTS:** 01698 266155. Major watersports centre 15km SE of Glas and easily reached from most of of Central Scotland via M8 or M74 (jnct 5 or 6). 200 acred loch and centre with instruction on sailing, canoeing, windsurfing, rowing and waterskiing and hire facs for canoes, Mirrors and Wayfarers, windsurfers and trimarans. Sessions: summer 9.30am-10pm; winter 9.30am-5pm. (30/CAMPING)

404
C3

CASTLE SEMPLE COUNTRY PARK, LOCHWINNOCH: 01505 842882. 30km SW of Glas off M8 at jnct 29, A737 then A760 past Johnstone. Also 25km from Largs via A760. Loch nr village is 3km by 1km and at the Rangers Centre you can hire windsurfers, dinghies, canoes, etc. Bird reserve on opp bank. Peaceful place to learn.

TIME CAPSULE, MONKLANDS: Report: 375/WHERE TO TAKE KIDS.

WHERE TO EAT OUTSIDE GLASGOW

✝ ✝ **BRAEVAL OLD MILL, ABERFOYLE:** 01877 382711. Just E of Aberfoyle on A873 for Pt of Menteith and Stirling. Small converted 'mill' on edge of golf course. Nick and Fiona Nairn's place. Probably Scotland's most sought-after meal since Nick's TV career took off and I for one, who never knows far enough in advance what I'm doing to get in here, haven't had the pleasure recently. Nick not flaming over the hot stove nowadays, but he has them well trained. It's just v good. Lunch and dinner Wed-Sat and Sun lunch. Weekday lunches easier.   EXP

405
D2

✝ **THE BLACK BULL, KILLEARN:** 01360 550215. 2 The Sq. Good-looking village, 30mins N of Glas betw L Lomond (Drymen) and the Campsies. Excellent pub food and conservatory restau. Good service (owners had hotel in US); waiters have ear pieces! Imaginative cuisine way beyond usual pub standard. Excellent puds. Live jazz. (37/HOTELS OUTSIDE TOWN, 134/KID-FRIENDLY)   MED

406
D2

✝ **BRAIDWOODS, nr DALRY:** 01294 833544. Off main A78 coast rd, take Dalry rd at Saltcoats, 6km along country rd: the Braidwood's whitewashed cottages and Keith's legendary cooking. This is better than most of Glas and much better value (incl wines). Wed/Sat lunch and dinner, and Sun lunch.   MED

407
C3

✝ **RISTORANTE LA VIGNA, LANARK:** 01555 664320. 40 Wellgate. Famously good Italian restau in a back st in Lanark. 7 days, lunch and dinner. Must book.   MED

408
E3

✝ **FINS, FAIRLIE, nr LARGS:** 01475 568989. On main A78 8km S of Largs, a seafood bistro, smokery, shop and craft/cookshop. This place is altogether good. Chef Gillian Dick uses exemplary restraint and the wine list is similarly to the point. Lunch and dinner. Cl Mon.   INX

409
C3

✝ **THE CROSS KEYS, KIPPEN:** 01786 870293. An inn that's been here forever in this quiet backwater town off the A811 15km W of Stirling. Bar meals by coal fire, à la carte and family restaus. A real pub food haven, and about the only thing Egon Ronay has got right around here. LO 8.45pm.

410
D2

✝ **WHEATSHEAF INN, SYMINGTON, nr AYR:** 01563 830307. 2km off the A77. Pleasant village off the unpleasant A77 with this busy

411
C4

coaching inn opp church. Folk come from miles around to eat (book at w/ends) honest-to-goodness pub fare in various rms (roast beef every Sun). Menu on boards. LO 10pm.

FOX AND HOUNDS, HOUSTON: Report: 233/PUB FOOD.

OTHER MUSTS

412
C3

✝ ✝ ✝ **NARDINI'S, LARGS:** 01475 674555. The Esplanade, Glas side. An institution. The epitome of the seaside cafeteria and all the nostalgia of Doon the Watter days. This airy brasserie with cake, ice cream and chocolate counters and in the back a trad tratt with full Italian à la carte and OK wines has a timeless formula which works today as well as it ever did. The light fittings, like almost everything else, are true originals. Summer evenings with the long light and a bowl of ice cream and the place busy with all kinds of folk is life-affirming stuff. Get you down there. High tea (4-6pm) is always a good idea. Summer until 10.30pm, winter until 8pm.

413
D3

TORTOLANO'S, UDDINGSTON: 29 Main St. 15km E of Glas via M74, Uddingston t/off, at the lights where you turn for Bothwell Castle (*see above*). Tiny confectioners/ice-cream shop with proper biscuit cones as an option and 5 flavours (try their 'double cream') all home-made by Montecassino's Mr Tortolano. Their loss, definitely our weight gain.

414
D3

COLPI'S, MILNGAVIE: Opp Black Bull in Milngavie (pronounced 'Mullguy') centre and there since 1928. Many consider this to be Glasgow's finest. Only vanilla at the cone counter but strawberry/chocolate flake/amaretto/honeycomb to take home. There's another branch in Clydebank. 7 days, until 9pm.

415
D3

✝ ✝ **FINDLAY CLARK, MILNGAVIE:** In Campsie country N of city, 20km from centre via A81 and A807 (Milngavie or Kirkintilloch rds) or heading for Milngavie, turn rt on Boclair Rd. Vast grd complex and all-round visitor experience – an institution. 'Famous' coffee shop (the famous waitresses tend to be local babes, but no means all of them), saddlery with everything except horses; labels from Crabtree and Evelyn to Fisons, plus books, clothes and piles of plants; and live pets. 9am-8pm (until 6pm in winter).

CARFIN GROTTO, MOTHERWELL: A723 just o/side Motherwell 4km from M8, on left after 2nd garage. A homage to Lourdes, built largely by striking miners in 1921. (God's) acre of grds and pathways with reliquaries, shrines, a glass pavilion and chapel. The ghost of Ravenscraig is always in the background. Spiritual sustenance, despite the throngs, for the true believers; something of a curiosity for the rest of us. Pilgrimage centre and tearoom. Open at all times.

416

E3

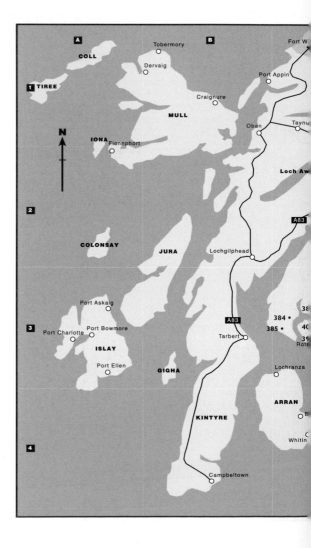

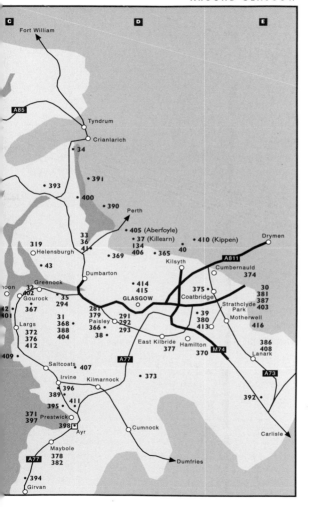

C
D
E

Fort William

A85

Tyndrum

Crianlarich

• 34

• 391

• 393

• 400

• 390

Perth

33
36
414

• 405 (Aberfoyle)
• 37 (Killearn)
134
406   • 365

• 410 (Kippen)

Drymen

40

319
○ Helensburgh

• 369

Kilsyth

A811

Cumbernauld
374

• 43

Dumbarton

• 414
415
GLASGOW

375 •

Coatbridge
○

30
381
387
403

noon
○
32
402
Gourock

Greenock

• 35
294

Strathclyde
Park

42 •
401 •

367

• 39
380
413○

Motherwell

416

Largs

31
368
388
404

281
379
Paisley ○
366 •
38 •

291
292
293

386
408
Lanark

372
376
412

East Kilbride
377

Hamilton
370

M74

A73

409 •

Saltcoats
• 407

A77

392 •

Irvine

389 •

396

• 373

Kilmarnock

395 •
411 •

371
397

Prestwick
○

398 ▣

Ayr

Cumnock

Carlisle

Maybole

378
382

A77

• 394
○ Girvan

Dumfries

SHOPPING GAZETTEER

This is a selection of useful shops that get it rt. South is S of a central area bisected by the river. E/W axis taken as Renfield St.

ESSENTIALS

Butchers

GILLESPIE'S, 1601 Gr Western Rd, Anniesland. 959 2015. WEST

JAMES ALLEN, 85 Lauderdale Gdns. 334 8973. WEST

MURRAY'S, 121 Royston Rd. 552 2201. EAST

Bakers

BRADFORDS, 245 Sauchiehall St and branches. 332 2057. CENTRAL

Bread: **BAKEHAUS,** 387 Gr Western Rd. 334 5501. WEST

Pâtisserie: **PÂTISSERIE FRANÇOISE,** 138 Byres Rd. 334 1351. 1351 Springburn Rd. 558 7377. WEST/EAST

Barbers

CITY BARBERS, 99 W Nile St. 332 7114. CENTRAL

SALANDINI'S, 342 W Princes St. 334 1064. WEST

Delicatessen

FRATELLI SARTI, 133 Wellington St. 248 2228. CENTRAL

PECKHAMS, 100 Byres Rd/Central Stn/Clarence Dr. WEST/CENTRAL/WEST

COOKERY BOOK, 20 Kilmarnock Rd. 632 9807. SOUTH

TOSCANA, 44 Station Rd, Milngavie. 956 4020. NORTH

LA TEA DOH, 126 Nithsdale Rd, Pollokshields. 424 3224. SOUTH

Kosher: **MORRISONS,** Sinclair Dr. 632 0998. SOUTH

Department Stores

FRASERS, 45 Buchanan St. 221 3880. CENTRAL

General: **DEBENHAMS,** 97 Argyle St. 221 9820. CENTRAL

Ironmongers: **CROCKETS,** 136 W Nile St. 332 1041. CENTRAL

Fishmongers

ALAN BEVERIDGE, 188 Byres Rd/7 Stn Rd, Milngavie. WEST/NORTH

FISH PLAICE, alley off Saltmarket by St Andrews St. 552 2337. EAST

MacCALLUMS, 944 Argyle St. 455 Gr Western Rd. 334 5680. WEST

Flowers

ROOTS AND FRUITS AND FLOWERS, 451 Gr Western Rd. 334 5817. WEST

Dried: **INSCAPE,** 141 Gr Western Rd. 332 6125. WEST

Fruit & Veg

ROOTS AND FRUITS, 457 Gt Western Rd. 339 5164. 355 Byres Rd. 334 3530. WEST

NO. 1 FOR VALUE, 61 Candleriggs, by City Hall. CENTRAL

Fish 'n' Chips

UNIQUE, 223 Allison St. 423 3366. SOUTH

PHILADELPHIA, 445 Gt Western Rd. 339 2372. WEST

UNIVERSITY CAFÉ, 83 Byres Rd. 334 9813. WEST

Hairdressers

RITA RUSK, 49 W Nile St. 221 1472. CENTRAL

DLC, Mitchell Lane. 204 2020. CENTRAL

ALAN EDWARDS, The Briggait. 552 5232. 56-58 Wilson St. 552 5282. EAST/CENTRAL

GARY'S CUTTING CLUB, 76 Drymen Rd, Bearsden. 942 0393. NORTH

Hats

PANDORA'S HATS, 5 Sinclair Dr, Battlefield. 649 7714. SOUTH

Late-night

General: **GOODIES (and others adj)** 645 Gt Western Rd. 334 8848. WEST

FRIENDLY'S, Elmbank St/Sauchiehall St. CENTRAL.

ALLDAYS, Kelvinbridge. WEST

Chemist: **MUNRO'S,** 693 Gt Western Rd. 339 0012. WEST

C and M MACKIE, 1067 Pollokshaws Rd. 649 8915. SOUTH

Lingerie

SILKS, 675 Clarkston Rd. 633 0442. SOUTH

PAMOAS LINGERIE 78 Hyndland St. 357 2383. WEST

Men's Clothes

New Labels:

CRUISE, 47 Renfield St. 248 2476. CENTRAL

SLATER MENSWEAR, 165 Howard St. 552 7171. CENTRAL

ITALIAN CENTRE, John St (Armani, Versace, etc). CENTRAL

Newspapers

NEWSPAPER KIOSK, Buchanan St. CENTRAL

BARRETTS, 263 Byres Rd. 339 0488. WEST.

International Magazines: **JOHN SMITH,** 57 St Vincent St. 221 7472. CENTRAL

Pasta

FAZZI BROTHERS, 67 Cambridge St/230 Clyde St. 332 0941. CENTRAL

FRATELLI SARTI, 133 Wellington St. 248 2228. CENTRAL

Shoes

Shoes That Last: **ROBERT JENKINS,** 183 Hyndland Rd. 334 8547. WEST.
14 Royal Exchange Sq. 248 3743. CENTRAL

Modish: **SCHUH,** 45 Union St. 221 1093. CENTRAL

ASPECTO, 20 Gordon St. 248 2532. CENTRAL

Tobacco

ROBERT GRAHAM & CO., 71 St Vincent St. 221 6588. CENTRAL

TOBACCO HOUSE, 9 St Vincent Pl. 226 4586. CENTRAL

Wholefoods

GRASSROOTS, 48 Woodlands Rd. 353 3278. WEST

QUALITY DELI, 123 Douglas St. 331 2984. CENTRAL

Wine

UBIQUITOUS CHIP WINES, 12 Ashton Lane. 334 5007. WEST

FRATELLI SARTI, 121 Bath St (also Wellington St, *see Pasta above*).
CENTRAL

PECKHAM AND RYE, 21 Clarence Dr. 334 4312. WEST

LITTLE ITALY, 205 Byres Rd. 339 6287. WEST

Women's Clothes

New Labels:

ITALIAN CENTRE, *as Men's Clothes above* (also Mondi). CENTRAL

CRUISE, 180 Ingram St. CENTRAL

MAXXI, 162 Fenwick Rd. 620 3133. SOUTH

MOON, 10 Ruthven Lane. 339 2315. WEST

Labels: **FRASERS,** 45 Buchanan St. 221 3880. CENTRAL

THE MOST INTERESTING SHOPS

One shopping precinct in Glas is referred to many times below,
namely **PRINCES SQUARE,** an indoor shopping mall off the middle of
Buchanan St (Argyle St end) and probably the single best concen-
tration of high-quality, interesting shops in town. These include
CHRISTIAN LACROIX, LUSH, SHEILA MILLER and **LINENS FINE.** For a coffee
break or snack, **D'ARCY'S** or **IL PAVONE** on the basement floor are just
fine.

Antiques

General: **HERITAGE HOUSE,** Unit 39, Yorkhill Quay. 5508770. WEST

LANSDOWNE ANTIQUES 334 8469 and **RETRO,** Otago St. WEST

Bric-à-Brac: **ALL OUR YESTERDAYS,** 6 Park Rd. 334 7788. WEST

Jewellery: **VICTORIAN VILLAGE, SARATOGA TRUNK,** 57 W Regent St. 332 0808. CENTRAL

Clothes: **STARRY STARRY NIGHT,** 19 Dowanside Lane. WEST

Art Supplies

MILLERS, Stockwell St. 553 1660. Dalhousie St. 331 1661. WEST.

ART STORE, 94 Queen St. 221 0266. CENTRAL

Baby Goods and Kids' Stuff

Clothes: **STRAWBERRY FIELDS,** 517 Gr Western Rd. 339 1121. WEST

Toys: **THE SENTRY BOX,** 175 Gr George St. 334 6070. WEST

Cards and Gift Wrap

PAPYRUS, 374 Byres Rd. 334 6514. 296 Sauchiehall St. WEST/CENTRAL

PHOENIX GRAPHICS, 254 Sauchiehall St. 353 0102. CENTRAL

ILLUMINATI, Princes Sq. 204 2361. CENTRAL

Ceramics

NANCY SMILLIE, Princes Sq. 248 3874. Cresswell Lane. CENTRAL/WEST

WARE ON EARTH, Italian Centre, Ingram St. CENTRAL

Clothes

General: See SHOPPING FOR ESSENTIALS and Princes Sq (above).

Hip: **MELLO,** 2659 Virginia St. 552 5656. CENTRAL

HUSTLER AND PENELOPE'S PITSTOP, Queen St. CENTRAL

Nearly New: **ALCHEMY,** 519 Gr Western Rd. 334 9610. WEST

Old: **BOEM SCIFRA,** De Courcey's Arcade, Cresswell Lane. 357 1335. WEST

FLIP, 68 Queen St. 221 2041. CENTRAL

THE SQUARE YARD, Stevenson St W at **THE BARRAS** (265/OTHER ATTRACTIONS). EAST

Outdoor: **BLACK'S,** 254 Sauchiehall St. 353 2344. CENTRAL

TISO'S, 129 Buchanan St. 248 4877. CENTRAL

CLEARWATER WORK & LEISURE, 1124 Argyle St. 334 2228. WEST.

Collectables

RELICS, Downside Lane. 341 0007. WEST

JADES, 1121 Maryhill Rd. 946 2920. WEST

KOLLECTABLES, 51 Parnie St. 552 2208. CENTRAL

Comics

FUTURESHOCK, 88 Byres Rd. 339 8184. WEST

FORBIDDEN PLANET, 168 Buchanan St. 331 1215. CENTRAL

Furniture

Modern: **INHOUSE,** 26 Wilson St. 552 5902. CENTRAL

TONY WALKER, 92 Woodside Terr. 332 2662. WEST

Traditional: **ADRIENNE'S,** 28 Park Rd. 334 5943. WEST

Games

GAMES WORKSHOP, 66 Queen St. 226 3762. CENTRAL

PC/Console Games: **C.A GAMES,** De Courcey's Arcade, Cresswell Lane. 334 3901. WEST **G FORCE,** 77 Union St. 248 8272. CENTRAL

Ice Cream

COLPI, Milngavie centre, Newton Mearns and Clydebank

QUEENS CAFÉ, 515 Victoria Rd. 423 2409. WEST

UNIVERSITY CAFÉ, Byres Rd. WEST

Interiors

DESIGNWORKS, 38 Gibson St. 339 9520. WEST

INHOUSE, 26 Wilson St. 552 5902. CENTRAL

Jewellery

ARGYLE ST ARCADE. Vast selection of different shops. CENTRAL

SHEILA MILLER DESIGNER JEWELLERY, Princes Sq. 221 1248. CENTRAL

Jokes

TAM SHEPHERD'S, 33 Queen St. 221 2310. CENTRAL

THE PARTY SHOP, 201 Sauchiehall St. 332 3392. CENTRAL

Junk

THE BARRAS (265/OTHER ATTRACTIONS). EAST

Presents

EVOLUTION, 396 Byres Rd. 334 3200. WEST

NICE HOUSE, Italian Centre, Ingram St. CENTRAL

PAST TIMES, 70 Buchanan St. 226 2277. CENTRAL

Sports

NEVIS SPORT, 261 Sauchiehall St. 332 4814. CENTRAL

BOARDWISE, 1146 Argyle St. 334 5559. CENTRAL

Tartan

Serious: **HECTOR RUSSELL,** 10 Buchanan St. 221 0217. CENTRAL

GEOFFREY'S, 309 Sauchiehall St. 331 2388. CENTRAL

Tacky: **ROBIN HOOD GIFT HOUSE,** 11 St Vincent St. 221 7408. CENTRAL

Theatrical Costumes

THE PARTY SHOP, 201 Sauchiehall St. 332 3392. CENTRAL

DRESS U UP, 1011 Argyle St. 221 2087. WEST

INDEX

Index

COLLINS

Other titles by Peter Irvine published by HarperCollins *Publishers* are:

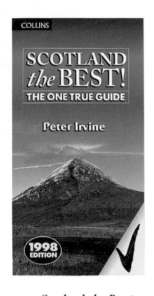

Edinburgh the Best!
ISBN 0 00 472152 7
£5.99

Scotland the Best!
ISBN 0 00 472150 0 (hardback)
£12.99
ISBN 0 00 472151 9 (paperback)
£9.99